# WELCOME

# TO

# HOPE!

(Revised, October, 2019)

Arden Thiessen

Previous Books by Arden Thiessen
*The Life of Faith,* 1984
*The Biblical Case for Equality,* 2002
*The Church that Christ Builds* (Ephesians), 2006
*Good News for a Broken World* (Romans), 2007
*Keeping in Step with the God of Peace,* 2008
*Hope for Tough Times* (1 & 2 Peter), 2009
*The Grace and the Glory* (Gospel of John), 2015
*Twenty Big Questions,* 2016
*In Praise of Altruism.* 2017
*Growing up with God,* 2018
*Living for Others,* 2019 (previously, *In Praise of Altruism*)

# Welcome to Hope!

## Contents

# Introductory Meditation

In October of 2017 we were driving across southern British Columbia on Highway #3. Near the city of Hope I was attracted to their bold welcoming sign, "Experience Hope." I had already for a few years been mulling over the idea of writing a book on hope and the sign seemed to flash the message, "Invite your friends to experience hope!"

So, this book will invite you to experience hope. However, humility and honesty remind me this invitation does not come from me; I am only its messenger. My invitation is extended to you by the almighty triune God, the Originator and Creator of everything that is. Hebrew believers spoke of their God as Jahweh, the personal God who had revealed himself to Abraham, Isaac, Jacob, and Moses. Those of us who accept the further revelation as it comes to us through the New Testament writings understand that Jahweh has appeared here in person, in the flesh, as a carpenter's son; they called him Jesus. Throughout the sacred writings that bring God to our attention, whether as Jahweh or Jesus, there are generous sprinklings of hope. To believe in the God who is revealed in the Holy Scriptures is to be surrounded by an aura of hope. I'm taking it upon myself now to discuss and explore these biblical invitations for the benefit of my reading friends.

To speak about an invitation to hope, by itself, seems like a half-finished idea. Hope for what? You can answer the question any way you like. Whatever is wrong, whatever is distressing, whatever fills you with guilt, whatever confuses you, whatever frightens or worries you, whatever causes you to wake up at night shaking with anxiety. God invites you to hope that it will be okay.

This is not going to be exhaustive; I will not say everything that could be said. This is supposed to be accessible and readable. However, I promise you it's going to be about hope all the way – I will not stray aside much, I hope, and I plan to promote hope as one of the basic essentials for healthy, successful living.

To present a preview of what to expect I mention theologian James K. A. Smith's five structural elements of any hope and I will give a Christian slant to them (pp. 207-9). First, there is the hoper. Without the Christian hoper there is no hope.

Second, there is the object that is hoped for. For the Christian, that might be as varied as hoping for the cure of one's cancer, the cessation of violence in the Arab world, the rescue and conversion of a delinquent daughter, an improvement in justice for the impoverished and marginal members of our society, or for the personal assurance of eternal life.

Third, there must be the act of hope. There must be a deliberate decision to focus by faith on the promises and possibilities and to live by them. True, hopeful faith will make a difference in the values by which one makes decisions.

Fourth, we must look at the ground of hope. For the Christian believer this is the existence of a gracious and loving God who has received us and promises to be with us and grant us what we need.

Fifth, we need to expect the eventual fulfillment of our God-given expectations. Hope is not a guarantee and it does not come with a schedule for its fulfillment. But it means counting confidently on God in all circumstances.

Now, here is a totally non-academic list of the reasons why one needs hope to live well. (Charles Swindoll has a similar list in the opening chapters of his conversational commentary on 1 Peter, *Hope Again*).

-Hope points us to the light at the end of the tunnel when we find ourselves trapped in the blackness of our present miseries and anxieties.

-Hope will give us energy to keep on plugging along when we are overworked and feel our strength to be ebbing away.

-Hope can lift our spirits into the brightness of the noonday when we are discouraged and are sinking into the darkness of despair.

-Hope can prompt us and prod us to keep on going when our duties seem meaningless and we are tempted to throw up our hands and simply quit.

-Hope can protect us from giving in to panic when we lose our way and are confused about the direction of the road ahead.

-Hope reminds us God will never abandon us when terrible news fills us with fear.

-Hope gives us the strength to admit our bad decisions and then to endure the consequences.

-Hope gives us the grace to be patient and wait for the Lord when unemployment, disabilities, illness, or other bad things seem to make our life useless.

-Hope guides us through the suffering of grief when we have said our final farewell to someone we love.

* * *

A gentle statement of confession may be in order before I proceed any further. I have wondered, will I write as a pessimist or an optimist? Over the years, I have noticed that I am rarely surprised when the bad thing happens. I've often muttered to myself, "I thought so; I *suspected* that would happen." Toronto sportswriter Cathal Kelly says for people with an Irish mentality, "A good thing is just the prelude to the bad thing coming around the corner." I don't have a drop of Irish blood in my veins but I sometimes catch myself thinking the same way. So, am I a pessimist? Maybe! However, the very fact that I felt moved to write about hope seems to say that I'm at least trying to recover from the problem and that I'm not a hopeless pessimist.

I am writing as a Christian believer for fellow believers. I decided that I could see this line from the apostle Peter as providing me with the basic theme for the book, "By his great mercy he has given us a new birth into a living hope through the resurrection of Jesus Christ from the dead" (1 Peter 1:3). The sentence tells us:

-We have hope because we have been born into a new life.

-God worked this out for us because of his great mercy.

-We have hope because we know God raised Jesus out of death.

-The hope we have received from God is a living hope.

A living hope is not a dead, static, inert, changeless entity. A living hope will keep on vitalizing us, growing with us, changing and developing as we live with it. My dream is that this book will do that for me as I write and for you as you read.

I did not want to give this writing too much of an academic feel. Consequently, quotations have only been noted with the author's last name and page numbers. Full bibliographic information on my sources can be found at the back of the book.

The biblical quotations I will use are from the New Revised Standard Version, unless otherwise noted. In case you haven't guessed yet, I have been soaking myself in the biblical data for a long time. Consequently, this book will likely have a biblical smell throughout – or should I be hopeful enough to call it an aroma?

I plan to use the Bible, not in a suffocating way to suppress all variant notions and ideas, but as an agent of enlightenment. I respect the Bible as the best possible source of truth and clear thinking that we have. However, there is in the Bible so much adultery and idolatry, the slaughtering of children and the degradation of women, revenge and punishment, violence and ferocity (sometimes apparently mandated by God himself), petty resentments and destructive fury (sometimes even modelled by God, at least as far as the record goes), that it almost drives me crazy. Clear biblical thinking seems to be miserably unclear. But I refuse to give up with the Bible, and in recent years I have been impressed so much by the goodness and the grace, the patience and the forgiveness, the kiss of welcome, the embrace of hospitality, and the benediction of infinite love that I notice all over the Holy Writings, that the ugliness seems to fade into the background. Does that mean I am now an apostate pessimist? I hope so! I now believe that it's all going to be OK, ultimately. And I think I smile easier than I used to.

I have no doubt that some readers will think hope is getting too much popular press in this book. I expect that the conservative religious concern to defend righteousness and not dilute the Word of God may keep some of us from hoping as strongly as this book suggests. That may especially be true in Chapter 10, which is my personal testimony about hoping for grace beyond the grave. Some people are terribly afraid of imagining God to be more gracious than he is. My early sermons from forty or fifty years ago show that I was once one of them. Today I am more afraid of making God too small, of describing his grace and goodness too much according to current popular concepts of criminal justice, or to concepts of righteousness that we have inherited from the Middle Ages. I have wondered, what would God think of the writer or preacher who makes him better than he is? Is such a possibility even possible? The whole thought is rather incredible, is it not?

We honor God by hoping even if we are not sure how to interpret the promises of Scripture. This reminds me of the Scottish minister George

MacDonald, who was a bit of a free thinker. A member of his family once responded to one of his grand hopes, "It all seems too good to be true." He answered, "Nay, it is just so good it must be true" (MacDonald, p. 10).

Anyway, some readers will not agree with everything I have written. Maybe very few will. There is always a danger with being public and open with one's beliefs. I have been called a heretic for much lesser aberrations from popular theology than I will reveal here.

Now for a bit of defensive work to settle the reader's shaky nerves: To begin with, I affirm that I believe in the Holy Trinity as the early church fathers defined God. I agree with their conviction that Jesus is to be understood as fully God and fully man. When I first submitted myself in faith and loyalty to Jesus I saw him essentially as my Lord and Savior. Today I see him also as my Friend and Companion. I hold to the traditional view of God's omniscience rather than to the newer concept that God cannot know what has not yet happened, as do my colleagues in the open theism movement. I believe that the radical reformers, sometimes labelled Anabaptists, had the most holistic view of discipleship in the changing theological milieu of the sixteenth century. Finally, after years of theological turmoil I have concluded that it is impossible for me to believe that God determines and controls everything. In other words, I do not write as a determinist. At the heart of this whole book is my belief in the consensual view (as Thomas Oden calls it) that God has given us the freedom to make our own choices and make our own mistakes rather than that everything has been predetermined by a prehistoric divine decree. It is this last point, especially, that gives meaning to life, that makes life interesting, and that keeps on challenging us to hope for the best.

# Chapter 1 – First Thoughts about Hope

*Hope is being able to see that there is light despite all the darkness.* – Desmond Tutu

*Hope springs eternal in the human breast.* – Alexander Pope

*We must accept finite disappointments, but never lose infinite hope.* – Martin Luther King, Jr.

*Hope deferred makes the heart sick, but a longing fulfilled is a tree of life* (Prov.13:12 NIV).

*For it was by hope that we were saved* (Rom. 8:24 TEV).

A dictionary article says "Hope is an optimistic state of mind that is based on an expectation of positive outcomes with respect to events and circumstances in one's life or the world at large." If we want to lighten that up a bit we can say it means to "expect some future blessing with confidence" or to "to cherish a deep desire with a trustful anticipation." It is commonly understood that the absence of hope means discouragement, dejection, and despair.

"Hoping, like loving and believing, is a particular way of 'intending' the future" (Smith, p. 205). In order to live well we must include a hopeful vision of the future in our worldview. Hope is as essential for our daily living as the air we breathe and the food we eat. Hope is an aspect of faith; it is faith directed at the future. In hoping we look away from the present situation, away from the problems and worries of the day and anticipate that someday it will be better. Sometimes we even look way out into the future, beyond the boundary of time, off into eternity, and expect that eternity will fix all things and that the final state will compensate for all the hardships of this life.

Hope is at the heart of human existence. For life to be livable there has to be hope. And hope can only blossom into its fullness within a Christian worldview. Hoping will not work effectively unless we allow Jesus to assume the central role of leadership in our lives. We should not try to attach hope to knowledge and morality as a *concluding* addendum. Hope is the *beginning* of all clear thinking about this life and the future. Our rational powers soon freeze into tedium and inertia unless they are constantly inspired by the vital, hope-giving presence of Jesus.

For the Christian there is no hope without God. The beautiful promises of the Bible alone have no power at all; they don't fulfill themselves. The promises are always contingent on God, who has the right to decide when and how the requests of the hoper will be answered.

Those who walk with God must be prepared for the long wait. The Hebrew formula for the long silence of God, which is used all over the Bible, is forty days (or forty years, depending on the situation). "Forty" represents the long grind, the long tedious trek, that often has no clear termination point. It is this feature of our walk with God that changes stubbornness into a virtue. The nature of God's ways means that we must stubbornly refuse to let go of our grip on hope, no matter what.

It is important to understand that we humans are seriously disadvantaged when it comes to hoping. We are limited by our lack of prescience. What do we know about the future? Humanly speaking we can only look at the history of the human story and try to draw some inferences from the records of the past that we then project into the future. Such futurology easily degenerates into wishful thinking. In this essay I will assume that for hope to have any value, for hope to give us direction about the future, we have to open ourselves to the words of God. Only God is our assurance that the promised future will come to pass. Our life in this world is somewhat like looking at the horizon. It looks like the end, but we know there is more beyond the horizon even though it is invisible to us. God has the vantage point from which to look beyond the horizon.

In recent years many biblical theologians have promoted the view that the Bible is actually one big story, one meta-narrative. I think this approach helps us appreciate the meaning of Christian hope. The Bible should not be seen merely as a collection of verses, as juvenile readers sometimes do. It should not be seen as a random collection of ancient documents, as critical scholars sometimes do. It is one big story. Properly understood, it reads like a story. There is a beginning, there is a plot, there is the drama and tension of development, there is a climax and a conclusion. The entire biblical narrative is future-oriented. Our hope is the expectancy that the drama that began with the "beginning" of Genesis 1:1, of which we are still a part right now, will culminate as God has foreseen that it will. In other words, one cannot hope unless one believes that God is, and that God will be able to guide the story of the world to the culmination that he has announced.

The universal human need for hope signals that something is seriously amiss. It suggests that humankind is somewhat like a ship suffering distress at sea. Hope is the SOS signal. A person would not need to hope if there were no current problems and no anxieties about the future. The SOS signal of hope says two things about us. First, we are aware that something is wrong and we believe there should be some solution to our woes. Second, we realize we have to look for a savior outside of ourselves. We need to be visited with help from some source out there, and so we search the horizon for signs of the help that is, as yet, not visible to us.

A good, strong, healthy hope can give us the sense that the future blessing is already ours today. We can enjoy the future before it happens. Just as the child enjoys the holiday at the lake weeks before it starts, just as the engaged couple will already enjoy their future life together as they plan the wedding, just as the laborer toils away at an unfulfilling factory job for decades but is able to grind it out because every evening he thinks of the freedom to travel and immerse himself in his hobbies once he will retire, so all of us can be energized and lifted up by events that have not yet happened. The eighteenth-century Irish poet Oliver Goldsmith even declared, "The hours we pass with happy prospects in view are more pleasing than those crowded with fruition."

Writing about hope may seem like a revolutionary exercise, because revolutionaries are always oriented on the future. Revolutionaries do not accept the past or the present as satisfactory. I will argue that an attitude of biblical realism will require us to do the same; God has promised he will make all things new. Not only that, I will argue that Jesus' call for volunteers for the new kingdom he was planting on earth meant that he was asking men and women to join God in his program of world revolution. That call has never yet been abrogated. True Christians are revolutionaries; they refuse to accept the present as a given.

God's promise of a new future is still outstanding; careful attention to the Old Testament Scriptures will show us that the messianic promise to the Jewish community already contained much more than the world has yet experienced. Even now, as in the first century, the challenge of the apostle Peter stands firm, "Always be ready to make your defense to anyone who demands from you an accounting for the hope that is in you" (1 Peter 3:15). And I hope every reader intends to do it the right way. "Do it with gentleness and reverence," is Peter's concluding advice.

$$* * *$$

I will now breeze through a series of positions on hope that I have noticed in recent years. I begin with the atheistic perspective of the famous skeptic, the American philosopher Richard Rorty, who died in 2007. I choose him from many others because many have tried to understand him (James K. A. Smith helped me with that) and have often quoted him. Further, Rorty is the grandson of the Baptist pastor and evangelical socialist Walter Rauschenbusch. I am fascinated by the evolution from grandfather to grandson because I watch my adult grandsons dealing with the theological legacy that I've tried to pass on. As a secular postmodernist and strict atheist Rorty still speaks of hope, advocating the possibility of creating a modern, liberal utopia, in which justice will rule. He seeks to construct a "social hope" for the world of the future. His associate Jurgen Habermas wrote that Rorty's hope had been that "someday my remote descendants will live in a global civilization in which love is pretty much the only law."

However, Rorty denounces the hopeful visions of the past. He sees them as but futile attempts to brighten and lighten one's life with a false and unrealistic phantasy. The Christian story can also be shown to be a false hope, a vain theory that offers no hope for contemporary society. He says it is actually based on hopelessness, the fatalistic "Christian" view that this world with its human mess is incurable. And so, Christians exchange hope for this world for a hope in "pie in the sky when we die." He faults such an otherworldliness as morally and politically debilitating.

If there is no more substance to the Christian hope than Mr. Rorty's caricatures depict then I should close down this writing right here and simply challenge you to go out there, grit your teeth, and make the best you can with what ever will be. However, I will continue to plod forward, trying to show that true Christian hope has an interest in bettering this present world *while* being deeply committed to the vision of a future spiritual eternal kingdom of perfect truth and righteousness. And then I will argue that our zeal for the first will dry up unless it's empowered, replenished, and inspired by the second vision.

Even as I continue to expound on the theme of hope I do admit there is such a state as false, baseless, unrealistic hope, a hope that is simply a subjective attempt to soften the pain of one's personal anxieties. Psychologists and counselors have recognized that people are often deluded by a false hope. Such a false hope may be based on an unrealistic view or a misguided interpretation of one's life situation. A false hope may eventually evolve into no hope. Later in this book I will discuss how many *religious* people have lost their hope because their hope was not based on a true concept of reality and because of a misguided, delusional interpretation of the Bible's promises.

A false hope may be destroyed when the unthinkable tragedy strikes. In other words, the sudden tragedy may overwhelm us with the unavoidable realities of life, sickness, and death and wipe out any hope we may have had. On the other hand, sometimes hope may actually revive when the crisis strikes home. A new intense need may open us to new creative possibilities; with the great need our minds may be exposed to new, hopeful possibilities for personal empowerment that we did not need to consider when life was easy and happy. The range of future possibilities and options may lead to a new sense of hopefulness.

Maybe it's the possibility of holding an empty, false hope that has given rise to the view that hope is a vice. You see, not everyone agrees that hoping is healthy and good for us. Some see it as an irrational weakness, as a flight from reality. They suspect it is an irrational diversion, which may give rise to irrational actions. Ancient Greeks had the myth about Pandora's box. In that box were all the evils that the gods wanted to use to torment humans. Foolishly, Pandora opened the box. Out came a horde of sicknesses, vices, and insanity, as well as hope. To us that legend is a surprise but to some ancient Greeks it made sense; the

Stoics aimed to cultivate a resolute stoical realism in which there was no place or need for hope. Looking ahead to better times was, to them, an ignoble weakness. The Greek political philosopher Thucydides treated hope with outright cynicism, as he did most of the other issues on which he opined. The philosophical writers of ancient Hinduism also saw hope as an evil. Latter-day Marxists have railed against *Christian* hope because it interferes with their crusade for revolutionary change. Christian hope is drugging the masses into passivism, they say. As Karl Marx opined, religion is the opium of the people.

Another common accusation against the practice of hope is that it doesn't take evil and injustice seriously enough. Christian hope has been denounced for having confidence in a better future, and especially for its testimony of trust in an eternal future of bliss. To the unbeliever this seems incredibly unrealistic. It is often put down as escapism, as a refusal to face the present crisis. I have said that hope shows we are aware of the troubles; hope is then the wager that the odds stacked up against us can be overcome by God's help. What we see in front of us is not the end of the track. There is more around the curve. As Carl Braaten has it, "Hope is not a denial of the facts, but a refusal to accept them as the court of final judgment. Likewise, a theology of hope takes evil seriously, precisely by anticipating a power which can more than match it" (p. 40).

Hope counts on new possibilities. It is not bound to precedents of the past. It assumes we are free to make our choices, that God is free to surprise us with his response to our calls, and that the future has not been unalterably determined and set in stone. Things can change. Hope implies that the current status quo is relative and refuses to accept an eternally sealed fate. What has always been, need not determine what will be. Hope challenges the dark view that the future is closed and it will not model its expectation of the future on the memories of the past. With God the new thing is always possible.

✳ ✳ ✳

Let's continue our musing about hope. First of all, on the practical level, health care people seem to agree that hope has the ability to help people heal faster and easier. Individuals who maintain hope when battling illness significantly enhance their chances of recovery. The communication of hope is important in health care because people who are unwell often assume that their condition is irreversible and that they have little chance of recovery. Health care providers who recognize the importance of hope in the recovery process and learn to promote hope in their patients by guiding them into healthy coping strategies will often witness significant physical and emotional improvement. Consequently, helping the patient to be more hopeful and optimistic is an essential component of holistic healthcare. From the 19th century English poet Samuel Taylor Coleridge, who was always sickly, we have this wise comment, "He is the best physician who is the most ingenious inspirer of hope." I understand the American Dr. Karl Menninger was often referred to as the "apostle of hope." Working in the field of psychoanalysis he stressed that hope is at the heart of the human life and an indispensable ingredient of personal therapy. Samuel Johnson, among all his wise commentary, offers this opinion, "It is worth a thousand pounds a year to have the habit of looking on the bright side of things."

There is a psychology of hope. When hopelessness says, "No Exit!" the voice of hope cries, "I see a way out." Not only do people who possess hope, and think optimistically, recover their health more rapidly than those who feel hopeless, they also have a greater *sense* of wellbeing in whatever state of unhealth they may be.

Some psychologists explain that we can, in a sense, manufacture our own hope. We can do that by setting realistic goals for ourselves and then creating a strategy for how the goals may be attained. In other words, hope may be the product of one's own mental willpower. Hopeful people are like the little engine that could; they keep on telling themselves "I think I can, I think I can, I think I can". And they do it!

One particular, somewhat esoteric, expression of hope is utopianism: "Utopia" is coined from two Greek words: *eu* ("good" or "well") and *topos* ("place"). The common literary imagination is that somewhere there may exist, or somehow people may create, a new world of perfect wellness, goodness, and happiness. Cynics have pointed out that maybe the origin of the word is *ou* ("no" or "not") and *topos* ("place"). In other words, there is no such place. One does not even need to be a cynic to realize that all human efforts to create a perfect world, whether by Marxists, capitalists, feminists, sexual libertarians, ecologists, racists, right wingers, or regressive conservatives have largely failed. Utopia does not seem to be within human reach. It always ends up being a "notopia." However, the frequent emergence of the utopian dream in literature, in the social sciences, in religion, and in political engineering may witness to the fact that humans are designed for a higher and a better life than the mess in which they are presently muddling along.

A version of utopianism for the personal life is perfectionism. This can be defined as a persistent, compulsive drive toward unattainable goals. Perfectionists cannot relax where they are; they are driven to improve and succeed, whatever the cost may be. They reject the normal realities and constraints of human ability. They cannot live with themselves unless they are the best. Imperfection is never an option for them. They have no use for being average. They cannot accept failures and the dread of failing may then render them ineffective and impotent. In other words, their addiction to perfection may freeze them into inaction because any necessary action brings with it the possibility of failure. They are suffering helplessly from a neurotic hopelessness.

Hope is not the same as optimism, although optimistic people will find it easier to look ahead in hope. Optimism is not, specifically, a Christian virtue. There may be theistic optimists and there may be atheistic optimists. To some extent optimism is an inherited character trait. Some people just have a natural tendency to expect the best outcome in any given situation. However, it is probably true that it can also be influenced by social factors, past experiences, family environment, and personal health. The common idiom used to illustrate optimism versus pessimism is that of a glass half full of water; the optimist sees the glass as half full and a pessimist says the glass is half empty. They are looking at the same glass. Can optimism be learned? Some people have told me they have deliberately thought themselves out of their innate pessimism; now they always see the sunny side of life. Since I have a few streaks of pessimism left in me I usually doubt such a confession. Probably we can agree that the ideal attitude would be a perfect state of *realism*, an outlook that is based only on the honest facts. But is that realistically possible?

A sturdy hope, a persistent looking ahead to an eternal future of bliss, is not, as some folks think, a form of escapism or wishful thinking. To the contrary, as David Ben-Gurion is reported to have declared, "Anyone who doesn't believe in miracles is not a realist." In a world in which God is active the hope in miracles is totally realistic. It is an important aspect of the Christian witness in this depressing world. Further, it is not true, as some people critically declare, that this "pie in the sky" philosophy makes people useless in the here and now. C. S. Lewis reminds us that the apostles of Jesus who shook up the pillars of the Roman Empire, the great minds of the Middle Ages that kept Europe from reverting to paganism, and the English Evangelicals who abolished the slave trade all left their mark on earth because they had a firm and hopeful vision of heaven in their minds.

To this we could now add that the incentive for spreading the concept of higher education for all, the inspiration for universal health and welfare programs, the worldwide scope of relief and development work, and the missionary movement that has brought truth and the Holy Scriptures to the farthest reaches of the earth was largely promoted by people who had a clear hope of eternity in their hearts. It wasn't that they worked to earn heaven, but that the hope of heaven inspired them to work for others. C. S. Lewis concludes, "Aim at heaven and you will get earth 'thrown in'; aim at earth and you will get neither" (*Mere Christianity*, p. 118). Lewis reminds us that something like this seems to be true in other spheres of life. Health is a good that all people appreciate. The best way to experience health is to forget about it and live. If one makes health the basic concern of one's life one is in danger of becoming a cranky hypochondriac. And maybe sickly and unhealthy to boot.

✳ ✳ ✳

Hope is a key concept in most major world religions, ancient and modern. Often the hoper is seen as believing in some future state of eternal bliss, whether for the individual or for the collective group. This hope will often be seen as the fruit or consequence of spiritual attainment.

In Hinduism the concept of "Karma" seems to be a version of hope. It is an integral aspect of their concept of reincarnation. Karma is not fate and it is not bestowed by the gods. It is the universal principle of cause and effect. In Hindu belief, actions have consequences, and while one's effort and work may or may not bear near term fruits, it will eventually, maybe in a future incarnation, serve the good. Humans have the freedom to create their own destiny in future incarnations. It is the totality of actions and reactions in this and previous lives that determine the future.

Wise, intelligent action produces karma. The accumulation of karma may not be immediately evident. It may be somewhat of an unknown reality until it returns in this or other lifetimes. To the non-Hindu observer, like myself, it seems that their hope of a better life in the future is very much related to how they have lived their past lives and how well they manage it now. The good life will sooner or later lead to bliss. They create their own hope. But it seems to me this could also be a very depressing philosophy of life, because the person today has no control over, and no way of dealing with, the evil they may have done in a previous life.

It is difficult to understand how Muslims can hope for earthly improvements. Their controlling worldview is that of a total determinism; everything is predetermined by Allah. How can there be hope when everything, the good and the evil, has already been determined autocratically before the beginning? From an outsider's perspective it would seem that the Muslim would then simply hope that one may be fortunate enough to have been destined for the good, prosperous, and blessed life.

The Muslim expectation of eternity is easier to understand. A dictionary article explains: "According to the Quran, the basic criterion for salvation in the afterlife is the belief in the oneness of God, Angels of God, revealed books of God, all messengers of God, as well as repentance to God, and doing good deeds. Though one must do good deeds and believe in God, salvation can only be attained through God's judgment." After listing the details of their heavenly hope, it summarizes, "According to Muslim belief, everything one longs for in this world will be there in Paradise." That is their hope.

It is not necessary to examine here the traditional nature of hope in the Hebrew mind, since that will receive full attention when we explore the origins of hope in the Old Testament. However, the Jewish world has recently experienced a crucial crisis of hope through the Holocaust in Germany. Where was God when the Nazi establishment tried to wipe Judaism off the face of the earth? In 1970 Emil Fackenheim admonished his fellow Jewish people to continue in hope. In view of the holocaust it is imperative that Jews hope, he says. To now give up on hope would be to give up on God and give the victory to Hitler posthumously. If they would stop hoping they will be lost and they must not grant Hitler the posthumous victory of having destroyed Judaism after all. In other words, he sees hope as essential to the continuation of Jewish life.

In the Christian faith hope is often seen as one of the basic theological virtues, along with faith and love (1 Cor. 13:13). In some writings hope is seen as a strong and confident expectation of a future reward for one's faithfulness. Other writings see hope as a trust and confidence in the grace and goodness of God and teach that it is only due to God's infinite love that we can expect to be blessed with an eternity of bliss. The Apostle Paul argued that hope is the context in which the gift of salvation may be received. After explaining that all of creation, including all of humankind, is waiting and longing for redemption he concludes, "For in this hope we were saved" (Rom. 8:24 NIV).

The Christian concepts of hope or despair have been immortalized in two literary masterpieces. The Italian Dante, describing the entrance of Hell, saw over it the words, "Lay down all hope, you that go in by me." In John Bunyan's *The Pilgrim's Progress* it is Hopeful who comes to comfort Christian while he stays in Doubting Castle.

Totally apart from any religious belief there has in recent years developed a study of the future, dubbed "futurology." There are highly learned people who have dedicated themselves to the task of trying to predict what the future will bring. Some are political strategists, some are sociologists, some are investment advisers, and some are novelists or filmmakers. At one point I started a file, collecting examples of futurism, but after fifty years of collecting the stuff I discarded the file as hopelessly useless. Most of it was already totally out of date anyway.

It would be a mistake to assume that Christian hope and secular futurology are identical. They may sometimes sound as if they are two versions of the same attitude. But a crucial difference is that secular dreams of the future center on the world's *becoming*, on the eventual climax of the process of evolution. The future in Christian hope arrives by the *coming* of God's kingdom. It is summed up in the prayer that Jesus taught his disciples when they joined his movement; they were to pray, "May your kingdom come; may your will be done on earth as it is in heaven" (Matt. 6:10 TEV). The kingdom had come to them in the arrival of Jesus, the Son of God. Now their calling was to pray, and to work, until the influence of the kingdom would transform the earth into the likeness of God's heaven. And with that I hope you are now ready to join me as we survey the biblical witness to the reality and necessity of hope.

## *For Further Thought and Study*

*1. Recall situations in which the only way to endure living was just to hang on to hope.*

*2. In how far do you agree with the thought that through hope one can even now enjoy the blessings of the future?*

*3. Where have you seen that hope boosted physical or mental health?*

*4. What examples of false hope have you noticed in your family, church, or community?*

*5. If you have discovered that you can teach yourself to be optimistic and hopeful explain how you do that?*

*6. What do you learn about hope from a study of Abraham's experience in Romans 4:13-21? How do you understand the concept of "hoping against hope" (v. 18)? Where have you experienced such a tension in your life?*

*7. Read Hebrews 6:13-20. What do you learn about hope? What is the basis for Christian hoping? What difference does this hope make in one's life?*

# Chapter 2 – The Biblical View of Hope

*I would say that hope is man's answer to God's silence.* – Jacques Ellul

*Hope-lessness is God-lessness, because both are future-lessness.* – Carl Braaten

*Hope binds us to the future and thus frees us in the present.* – D. W. Gill

*Keep your voice from weeping, and your eyes from tears; . . . there is hope for your future, says the LORD* (Jer. 31:16, 17).

*May the God of hope fill you with all joy and peace in believing, so that you may abound in hope by the power of the Holy Spirit* (Romans 15:13).

Hope connects us with the future. Some theologians have in recent decades taken to speak of "the God of the future." With this they mean not only that God is a forward-looking God, not only that he repeatedly sets before us a vision of what is to come, but that God is also the power who will bring the promises of the future into reality. In this chapter we will discover that hope was an essential aspect of the life of faith and obedience that was expected of God's people at the beginning under the first covenant.

The Old Testament has many Hebrew words that can be translated as hope. These words communicate two kinds of "hope" themes. First there is the theme of confidence, of counting on God, of leaning on the Lord in trustful rest. In Psalm 78:5-7 the singer remembers that the Lord designated parents to teach their children "so that they should set their hope in God and not forget the works of God." Jeremiah sings about the present hope that connects us with God here and now, "Blessed are those who trust in the Lord, whose trust is in the Lord. They shall be like a tree planted by waters" (Jer. 17:7). This hope word expresses a general sense of confidence in the Lord.

The other "hope" theme is that of expecting specific help, as in Ruth 1:12 and Job 14:7. Very often this trait of hopeful expectancy is expressed in terms of "waiting" for some help to arrive (Ps. 27:14; 37:7, 9, 34; 130:5; Isa. 40:31; Micah 7:7). I see around twenty examples of this in the Psalms alone. That the attitude of prayerful, expectant trusting is so frequently called a "waiting" should remind us that living with God requires patience.

In spite of what I have just presented about the "hope" language of the Old Testament, it seems to me the writers were not keen on discussing the nature of hope as a quality of the godly life or developing hope as a psychological virtue. The Old Testament writings do that with the queue of trustful believers that they line up before us. Let's see what we can learn from them.

The entire Old Testament is a story of hope. However, the task of understanding and appreciating that hope has seemed immensely difficult to many recent thinkers. I create a context for this discussion by mentioning the insights of the respected French sociologist Jacques Ellul. Writing in 1972, he reflected on the religious scene in Europe and spoke darkly about God's silence (p. 176). What he means with this term is that God has not been speaking to humankind in modern times as he did to the ancients whose stories are recorded in the Holy Scriptures. He speaks of the "dreary silence of God" and of "our loneliness before a closed heaven."

Before I discuss Jacques Ellul's painful sense of God's silence any further, I remind you that the prophet Isaiah in his day already felt that God had gone into hiding. But in spite of that he would wait and hope, "I will wait for the Lord, who is hiding his face from the house of Israel, and I will hope in him" (Isa. 8:17). Later comes the painful lament, "Truly you are a God who hides himself, O God of Israel, the Savior" (Isa. 45:15). That sad confession has now become the complaint of modern humankind, Ellul says. But still he challenges us to look hopefully to the silent God and wait for him. Hope refuses to let the current emptiness and silence rule the day. Hope is the confession that binds us to this silent God. When the modern philosophical arguments seem to have demolished all trace of God, hope insists on shouting, "Let's wait and see."

Hope can actually be seen as an indictment of the silent God; in hope we refuse to believe that he is *not* there. Ellul concludes, "When man picks up the conversation in order to force God to speak, when he never leaves off crashing God's silence, when he refuses to put up with God's going back on his word, when he lets his hope burst forth, that is when he is obeying the Word of God" (p. 189).

According to Ellul, hope can be seen as violence. Jesus once said of the kingdom of God, "The violent take it by force" (Matt. 11:12). With that he may have meant to challenge his disciples to grab hold of the kingdom even if they could not yet understand it. Seize it in the hope that clarity will come. Such a stubborn hope was already demonstrated in early times by Job who refused to believe that the calamities that enveloped him could *really* be the totality of what God willed for him. After the long painful, miserable lament of 19:1-22 he still is inspired to shout out, "I know that my Redeemer lives, and that at last he will stand upon the earth; . . . then in my flesh I shall see God" (Job 19:25, 26).

* * *

In the Scriptures Abraham stands out as one who radically models what it means to adjust one's life on the basis of God's promises. We could see Abraham's experiences as the inauguration of biblical futurism. He was called to move away from his homeland, way out into the unknown. He obeyed God's call to move from his people, his family, his traditional home, and his security to a land where he would be seen as an outsider and an alien. He moved because he had heard God's call, "Go from your country and your kindred and your father's house to the land that I will show you." He obeyed the gut-wrenching order because of the promise, "I will make of you a great nation, and I will bless you, and make your name great, so that you will be a blessing" (Gen. 12:2, 3). That was all. No details, just the promise.

As the apostle Paul, in Romans, preaches the new hope that is ours through Jesus Christ he recalls how it was with Abraham. Abraham had not *earned* God's attention. The promise of greatness and blessedness and being a blessing rested on grace (Rom. 4:16). Later there was the repeated promise that Abraham and his wife, both senior citizens, would have a son. Abraham believed the Lord, and his actions showed that he believed *in* the Lord (Gen. 15:6). As Paul discusses the spiritual pilgrimage of Abraham he moves easily from faith to hope. Abraham hoped against hope (Rom. 4:18). That paradoxical expression suggests that believing was a struggle; Abraham struggled because there was very little tangible evidence that any of the Lord's noble words could possibly come true. However, Paul concludes, "No distrust made him waver concerning the promise of God, but he grew strong in his faith as he gave glory to God, being fully convinced that God was able to do what he had promised" (Rom. 4:20, 21). That is the apostle's vision of how it should be for us as we reflect on the meaning of Jesus.

Ellul explains that the gods of the ancient nations revealed themselves and then became idols. But the God of Israel never shows himself. All that is ever seen of him are but symbols, such as the three visitors who came to Abraham or the voice out of the burning bush that Moses heard or the cloud by day and the pillar of fire by night that the Israelite pilgrims followed as they trekked out of Egypt.

However, the God of Israel speaks and he gives himself a name. He opened up for his chosen people a "religion of the name" (Ellul, p.173). He speaks and his word is a promise. In fact, the name itself was a promise. When Moses heard the voice out of the burning bush speak to him about the distresses of his people back there in Egypt he wondered whose voice it could be. (He had been educated in the religions of Egypt and the gods of Egypt all had names). The voice answered "I am who I am." Hebrew scholars say that pithy phrase could be understood as meaning "I will be who I will be." The voice identified itself with the past; "I am the God of Abraham, Isaac, and Jacob." Then the voice turned to the future, "This is my name forever, and this is my title for all generations" (Ex. 3:1-15). That phrase of identification was condensed into the four-letter name, JHWH, which the Hebrew people articulated as "Jahweh." This was their name for their personal God (Most of the English versions that I use print that name as LORD; an exception is *The New Jerusalem Bible,* which consistently uses Jahweh).

That event at Horeb had immediate and direct implications for the people of Abraham. Not anymore was the religion of their Jahweh only a source of solace in their abject slavery; it inspired them to rise up and march away from the bondage. They followed the call of Jahweh into the unknown future. Not only did their LORD give them a handle for their own faith as distinct from Egypt's religions, the LORD inspired them to political dissidence and the assertion of their right to be free. As the LORD says in Leviticus 26:13, "I broke the bars of your yoke and enabled you to walk with heads held high (NIV)." Their exodus was a concrete response to the call of Jahweh, the God of the future. Eventually that exodus became a symbol, celebrated till today as a model of how God's people are always the children of hope, following God away from the slavery of the past into a God-given freedom.

Their God did not provide them with a holy site, he did not present himself as a visible figure to be idolized, he wanted them to remain a people of the way. As with Abraham at the beginning of their story, so now with Abraham's descendants. He called them to move on, to trust, to follow, and to keep their eye on the goal he held before them.

Probably the event that tested Jewish faith and hope as no other was the downfall of Jerusalem to the Babylonian onslaught and then the forced exile of their cultural leaders to Babylon, seven hundred miles away. There they sat in their abandonment. They had assumed Jerusalem would be invincible. After all, it was Zion, the city of God. They had feverishly prayed for help and organized themselves against the ruthless attackers. They lost. The city walls were demolished, what wealth was left was looted, the temple was destroyed and its precious artifacts were seized by the invaders. The Bible gives us a clear picture of their inconsolable grief as they reflected on their plight. God had failed them. What now? What does one do when one's highest confidence has been shattered? Into their disillusionment God's prophets spoke hope. Ezekiel, who was one of the captives, cried out, "Thus says the Lord God: I will gather you from the peoples, and assemble you out of the countries where you have been scattered, and I will give you the land of Israel" (Ez. 11:17). Jeremiah of Jerusalem, who had presciently warned the people of Judea that they would have to come to terms with the Babylonians because God would not protect them, later wrote to his exiled brothers and told them God's promise now was, "I know the plans I have for you, says the Lord, plans for your welfare and not for harm, to give you a future with hope" (Jer. 29:11).

The strongest message of hope for the depressed exiles came through the message that the book of Isaiah presented in chapters 40-55. By then, the Jewish exiles faced a new threat. They had come to terms with their confined life in Babylon. But now an ominous new danger loomed over their peace in Babylon. The Persians from the east were amassing their armed forces and seemed to be on the verge of invading and destroying Babylon. If that should happen, what would happen to the Jewish communities? Isaiah chastised them for their fear (Ch. 41). In the midst of their panic he announced three powerful words of encouragement (41:8, 9). First, God still saw them as his servant. In spite of their long history of faltering loyalty, God's election had never been abrogated. Second, God had chosen them. Their relationship to the God of Abraham had not just happened. They may not have understood it, but God's choice meant they mattered to him. Thirdly, God assured them they had not been cast off. For seventy years or so, they had wondered what their miserable defeat might be telling them. What was the meaning of that military debacle back then? Had they just imagined they belonged to God? Had the God who once chose them now disowned them? For these trembling survivors God has a clear and bracing promise, "Do not fear, for I am with you, do not be afraid for I am your God; I will strengthen you, I will help you, I will uphold you with my victorious right hand" (41:10).

They were given no formula for how to avail themselves of God's help. There was no information what the outcome would be. There was just the assurance, "I, the LORD your God, hold your right hand" (40:13). Therefore, there was hope, and no need to fear.

The good result of the Persian invasion, as we now know, was that the Persian rulers favored their Jewish citizens and encouraged them to move back home and rebuild their ruined city. Emil Fackenheim, whose clarion call of hope to his fellow Jewish people I mentioned above, explains that the Ten Tribes who were earlier defeated and dragged into exile by their Assyrian conquerors vanished and were lost. They were assimilated into the people that had subdued and defeated them because nobody was there for them with a promise from God. They could not resist the seductive pressures of the powers that had overcome them because they had no hope. The later exiles in Babylon persevered in their loyalty to the covenant because they had Isaiah, Jeremiah, and Ezekiel to preach hope.

The Old Testament teaches us to reject the suspicion that God has rejected us. Hope is the opposite of resignation to fate, of submission to the diabolical schemes of the evil enemy. It is the shield against danger, defeat, discouragement, and despair. This is the hope that was demonstrated by the three young men whose stories we read in Daniel 3. They declared, "Our God whom we serve is able to deliver us from the furnace of blazing fire and out of your hand." But then they stubbornly add that even if God should seem to let them down and not save them they will still not worship the king's image (3:17 18). This is rugged, obstinate hope; even if God would not "come through" as they knew he could and as they hoped he would, they would still hold to him and count on him.

Hope insists that God's promise must, and will, be kept. In hope we remind God that he has to keep his word. All this reminds us that hope is the central essential of faith in God. The innermost essence of the faith of the Hebrew community was anticipating the future that God would bring to them. Likewise, we cannot today settle down comfortably in the status quo. Loyalty to our God means we are always in the tension between present unfulfillment and the expectation of fulfillment. As theologians often say, in this world we are always somewhere between the "already" and the "not yet."

The Bible's consistent message of hope comes to a climax with the arrival of Jesus to his human family in Nazareth. His coming was like an exultant shout of hope for all of humankind as well as for the entire natural universe. God is still out there, in front of us, beckoning us to move forward with him. As Karl Barth put it, in the coming of Jesus "God has crossed over to man's side." And so now, like the stubborn woman in Jesus' parable (Luke 18:1-8), we keep on shouting in God's ears, "Hear us, our Lord! We insist, in Jesus' name, that you pay attention to our cries, because we have the right to expect your help."

Jesus did not mention hope specifically, but he did teach his followers to expect God's care (Mt. 6). And he made promises, that he will be with them right to the end of the age, that he will send the Holy Spirit to guide them, that they will do greater works than he did, and that he will come again.

In summary then, the Bible reminds us that this life of the present cannot be understood unless we accept God's vision of the future. The end gives meaning to the present as well as to the confused wanderings of humankind in the past. The entire biblical narrative is sprinkled with hints, suggestions, and promises that the story of humankind on earth will end well. Because of God's consistent loving presence throughout the human story, because we can trace the steps by which God has led his people from the beginning till now, we have confidence in the ability of God, and in his good plan, to achieve his promises from here on as well. In this hope we can already speak of the triumph of hope. It was the initial coming of Jesus the Messiah, prepared for by the history of Israel and then announced to the world by the apostolic community, that produced a hope that leads us in triumph over all earthly despair. That triumph is nowhere more confidently expressed than with the words of Titus 2:13, "We wait for the blessed hope and the manifestation of the glory of our great God and Savior, Jesus Christ." That will consummate it all. And with that we leave this chapter; the specifics of the New Testament's hope teaching will be used as the basic material for the following chapters.

### For Further Thought and Study

*1. What do you think of Ellul's concepts of hope and God's silence as the author reports it?*

*2. Israel responded to God's call by marching out of Egypt, where have you responded in hope and moved ahead into the unknown?*

*3. If you have ever felt betrayed and forsaken by God as Israel did after the fall of Jerusalem, how did you find the strength to continue in the faith?*

*4. Notice the gloomy darkness of Isaiah 8:17-22 and then read the exultant song 44:1-8. With what kind of promises does God try to pull them out of despair?*

5. *How do you make sense of the obstinate faith of the three Hebrew youths, that even if God would not help them they would still hold on to God (Dan. 3:16-18)?*

6. *What is it like to hold on to God when it seems as if he has forgotten or ignored you?*

7. *In view of the strong emphasis on hope in Psalms and the prophets, why did Jesus not preach specifically on hope? How did he do it indirectly?*

# Chapter 3 – Obstacles to Hope

*What is hope? Nothing but the paint on the face of Existence. The least touch of truth rubs it off.*
-Lord Byron

*Something was dead in each of us, and what was dead was hope.* – Oscar Wilde

*My hope is fixed strongly in Him, that you will heal all my infirmities (Ps. 103:3) through Him who sits at your right hand making intercession for us (Rom. 8:34). If this were not true I would despair of hope.* – Augustine of Hippo

*He breaks me down on every side, and I am gone, he has uprooted my hope like a tree (Job 19:10).*

*Against all hope, Abraham in hope believed and so became the father of many nations just as it had been said to him* (Rom. 4:18, NIV).

It will not be easy to maintain a robust hope in the current intellectual environment. In the past, the vision-casters in our Western culture tended to have a sunny, idealistic, utopian view of the future. The materialistic and intellectual conditions of the world had been on a steady incline for centuries and there was every reason to expect that this upward trend would continue. This upward trend in the process of social evolution was expected to carry on and gain momentum. Both we and our environment will keep on getting better and better, we were promised.

In the current social milieu the future is treated with a great deal of ambiguity. We are now frequently reminded that society was never as healthy as we had imagined. The nefarious propaganda campaign that George Orwell so effectively dissected in his classic parable *Animal Farm,* depicting the crookedness and duplicity of the Russian

Communistic system, has actually been practiced around the world by all civil regimes. We have been hoodwinked into believing that we were better off than we were. And we are not sure in which direction the future will take us. In fact, recent surveys show that the majority of younger people in North America do not expect they will be as healthy, wealthy, or comfortable as their parents were. Hope is now a rather fragile reality.

Another aspect of our culture that inhibits our social hoping is that the principles and values of the Christian faith matter less and less to our cultural colleagues. This means that to retrieve and retain our hope we will have to be ruggedly counter-cultural. For some of us that is not a new stance; we are used to it. Others, with their efforts at hoping, will feel like orphans in a crowd of strangers. The thesis of this book is that there can be no real and lasting hope without God. We need to accept that and try to live by it even though most of our social contemporaries will see such a view as meaningless babble.

The daunting task before us then is to identify the natural hopelessness around us, crystallize clearly what is *our* hope, and then witness to that hope by the way we live and speak. We will need to learn our own hope language. We need the strong confidence that grounding our hope in Christ will stand the test of time, but express our vision of the future with a careful humility. Can a hope grounded in God speak intelligently to the secular human who is grounded in an ambiguous, miserable, messy earthly shadow land? I will argue that it can, and that it is our duty to do so. We must be prepared to witness to our hope with grace even though it looks to our listeners as vapid nonsense. Somehow, we must navigate carefully between arrogantly claiming to know it all and the futile emptiness of knowing nothing. Our vision of a future of hope must be informed by transcendence, faith, imagination, and the values of our communal existence. This is the calling of the church of Jesus Christ.

\* \* \*

A major obstacle to hope in our times is the growing awareness of the fragility of our natural environments. There is a general and pervasive sense that we are living in risky times. What's really unnerving is that nobody seems to know exactly how deeply the risks run. The earlier culture of tough endurance has given way to a culture of uncertainty. This uncertainty stifles hope, both at the personal and at the social level. Various recent surveys show that many people think we have already done irreparable harm to our environment. All this is sobering because hope is an indispensable component of the cultural capital that is essential for human comfort, progress, and flourishing. The problem is that the technological revolution provides us with way more data about the state of our earth than one's mind can compute and comprehend. This leaves us with a sense of "where are we at anyway?" Everything looks as transient and disposable as the ubiquitous bathroom tissue.

Clear thinking about the environmental problem is hampered by a type of manic hopelessness that shows up occasionally in the media. There are social activists whose imagination is mesmerized by the thrill of an impending apocalypse. Such are not genuine environmentalists. They are not paying sincere attention to true science but seeing, in the current dilemma, an opportunity to degrade people with their fear mongering. One such case, reported by the media in July of 2018, is the new book by the New York professor of English literature John Scranton. In *We're Doomed. Now What?* he answers his own question by proclaiming that the earth and humankind is doomed. He says the only sensible response to the impending doom is to commit suicide; if you really want to save the planet you should die (I don't see the connection between my dying and the state of our planet). My response to this type of fatalistic sensationalism is to resort to a bit of gallows humor and observe that people, at least, are totally biodegradable. There are two types of unhealthy responses to such exaggerated doomsaying. First, there are those who are so troubled by this gloom that they throw in the towel with the grim conclusion that since it will all shut down quite soon anyway, we might as well just continue to live as we jolly well please. Secondly there are those Christians who see hope in all this gloom; for them this is another sign that the coming of Jesus is right at hand.

Late in 2018 some climatologists drew a clear line in the sand. It is 2030. Unless we stem the increasing warmup of the earth, 2030 is the year when we will be inundated in a global climatological chaos of unimaginable horror. We read this gloom and wonder, is this true science or is it faddish fear mongering?

Another obstacle to hope is archaism, the nostalgic fascination with a time that is past. Some people long for the lost past instead of anticipating a new future. Instead of speculating how the future utopia may be attained (which is to be applauded), they glorify the past and celebrate it as "the good old times." This happens in politics as well as in religion. The fact is there never has been an era of unqualified glory. Some of my theological colleagues celebrate the church of the first few centuries as if that was a golden age. Catholics long for a return to the high theology of the Middle Ages. Lutherans continue to admire Luther for his courageous convictions and the Reformed still relish the theology of John Calvin. In the Anabaptist tradition, in which I feel most comfortable, we honor the sixteenth century radicals who were a pain in the neck for Catholics, Lutherans, and Reformed alike. Back then we were the people who stood up for the total truth and followed Jesus as nobody else did, as some of our professors have been reminding us. However, there were flaws in every tradition. The myth of the golden past should be abandoned. It never was.

It is, of course, necessary to *remember* the past. God was at work then as well as now. But we cannot go back to the past. We should appreciate it, study it, learn from it, but then turn from it and walk forward. Veneration for the heroes of the past must not deter us from now following Jesus into the future. I know there is a certain security in sticking with the way things have always been done; every progressive pastor has discovered that, to his painful chagrin.

The Romanian historian, the late Mircea Eliade, has written extensively about the "myth of eternal return." This myth says only what is perennial is real; only what is repeatable is meaningful. Only what was valid in the past is valid today. We must look for answers to today's problems among the precedents of the past. The symbol for this worldview is the circle. What once was always comes around again. This is somewhat like the worldview of the ancient Greeks. This is the social version of the doctrine of personal reincarnation. One is in bondage; there is no escape from the Ferris wheel of life. All effort is then expended on trying to catch up with the past. The high priest of this mythical religion of the past is the historian. The Hebrew people were taught by their inspired prophets to long for, pray for, and wait for the new things of the future. This linear view of the human story was confirmed by the teaching of Jesus who suggested no one uses a new patch to mend an old garment (Matt. 9:16). In other words, the kingdom of God was not another patch on the old quilt; it was new. He preached an eschatological gospel. The past was important but we cannot return to it. The present is real but we cannot stay here. Always before us is the future, helping us to interpret the past and giving us direction in the present. Carl Braaten concludes, "Man is an experiment in the laboratory of history whose goal, according to the Christian hope, is new life in a new world" (p. 46). I will pay more attention to this new world life in the later chapters of this book.

* * *

From environmental apocalypticism as a hope-squelching feature of our times I turn to its religious counterpart, Biblical apocalypticism (the term comes from the Greek title of the last book of the Bible and is used to identify fearful and terrorizing natural events). Because there have been terrible natural events in the past and because Jesus predicted that the end times would be ushered in with further outbreaks of terror, efforts to foresee them and give dates to their timing have proliferated. Countless books have been written to predict what is unpredictable. The record of their success at dating the time of the "great tribulation" and the "second coming" of Jesus and the "end" of the world is pathetic. So far, they have all been wrong. The mistakes of the past – some of which just look plain stupid – make all thinking about the future suspect. The radio broadcasts, the TV programs, and the books that these false prophets have produced have resulted in deep skepticism about all Christian futurism. I keep on hearing ministers admit that they pay no attention to this future talk and never preach on it. One of worst examples of what I am describing was the Y2K debacle at the end of 1999. Those who simply ignored all the dire talk fared best.

Scrounging around to find what others had written about hope I found Anne Lamott, who sometimes uses bad language but writes with incredible humor, grace, and hope. Right after that I found Anne Graham Lotz, Billy Graham's daughter (Billy once said she was the best preacher in the family). Her language is scrupulously clean but she majors on the horrible. She writes about the genocidal massacre of the Holocaust, the killing fields of Cambodia, the tribal butchery of Rwanda, the eradication of intellectuals and the educated under China's Cultural Revolution and then declares, "The persecution of Christians yet to come will make all other bloodletting combined seem pale in comparison" (*The Vision of His Glory*, p. 148). Yes, she wrote that. In a book that ostensibly deals with hope! I hope I may have a little trace of the grace expressed by the first Anne and be preserved from the depressing pessimism of the second.

What I have written above reminds me of a strange trait I have noticed among some evangelical people. They seem to have an obsessive craving for bad news. They relish the gloom. *Good* news about world issues actually seems problematic to them. The world is supposed to be getting worse, not better. According to their worldview, it is when life will become unspeakably horrible that Christ will come. So, the worse it gets the brighter their future looks. There are writers who assume the same; they think the worst possible scenarios they can create about the future will best serve their readers. They see it as their calling to invite people, or scare people, into heaven by making the earthly future as horrible as possible.

The obstacles to faith that I have listed are augmented and reinforced by the realities of life around us. Maybe this is the greatest problem of all. As Rabbi Kushner wrote years ago, bad things actually happen to good people. We see it in our own lives and among the people around us. There are no exemptions. Bad things keep on happening even to the most devout, in spite of their faith and their faithful praying. How can one then keep on hoping for the good?

This ongoing tension between hope and the agents of despair is graphically exemplified by the experiences of the Israelite people during their wilderness pilgrimage to the land of promise. They grew weary of hoping and began to despair of the future. When they could not see any escape from the dense wilderness of despair in which they were stumbling about, they cried for a return to the past. They lost confidence in Jahweh, the God whom they only knew by name. Their need for a visible, physical god was so intense that they convinced Moses' brother to provide them with a gold calf that would guide them on. They had further spells when they longed for the security of Egypt's slave gangs rather than the intangible promise of a land of milk and honey somewhere out in the north east.

The stories of those travails of faith during the years in the wilderness were never forgotten by the Israelite people. Instead, they were enshrined in their worship material (See Psalms 78, 105, 106, 135, 136). The inspired poets who developed those Psalms knew all about those historical problems. They never tried to evade them or wish them out of existence. But they received the grace to see the hand of God in the worst of the stories that they pulled out of their collective memory. Times had been bad, their ancestors had acted with little faith, but God had been good throughout. That assurance encouraged them to hope for the best in their future. We need to learn from them. Let us clearly and candidly admit the hurts and disappointments that follow us around throughout our days, but then trust the good and gracious God of the past to create for us a beautiful and blessed future.

### *For Further Thought and Study*

*1. Of which of the obstacles that the author discusses have you been aware? How has it affected your view of the future?*

*2. Which other discouraging features of our common culture could the author have presented?*

*3. What have you noticed, in your personal life or in the human experiences in the world around you, that has tended to diminish your hope?*

*4. Study Psalm 78:5-35 and look for the following:*
*-Why is it important for children to set their hope in God (v. 7)?*
*-What do you learn about God from this text?*
*-Notice and list all the responses that God expects from his people.*
*-Browse through the other Psalms mentioned above for more insight into the Israelite experiences of discouragement and hope.*

*5. Israel made a tragic mistake when they lost confidence in God's promises. Read about their fateful request for an idol god (Exodus 32). Where have you been similarly tempted? What helped you to overcome?*

# Chapter 4 – Hope and Providence

*Hope is nothing else than the expectation of those things which faith has believed to have been truly promised by God.* – Jurgen Moltmann

*I am ceaselessly torn between the goodness of God and the affliction of humankind, and the link between the two.* – Simone Weil

*Not that I am (I think) in much danger of ceasing to believe in God. The real danger is coming to believe such dreadful things about him.* – C. S. Lewis

*No good thing does the Lord withhold from those who walk uprightly* (Psalm 84:11).

*And my God will fully satisfy every need of yours according to his riches in glory in Christ Jesus* (Phil. 4:19).

This chapter continues the theme of the previous – dealing with the obstacles to hope that we encounter constantly. The theme of this chapter is probably uppermost in the minds of most hopers, rather than the philosophical or social issues discussed in the previous chapter. We live here in a world that is dreadfully flawed. What we see, hear, and experience gives us little reason to hope for better times. All hope counts on God's providence. But how can we trust in God's providential care when the media assaults us every evening with sickening news and gruesome pictures of floods, tornados, earthquakes, tsunamis, volcanic eruptions, forest fires, and the droughts that may force millions to live on the edge of starvation. Is there any evidence that the universe is managed by a God who cares about people?

Worse yet, humans who have been designed to care about each other and live in communities of compassion and love, and could do that if they chose to, regularly shock us with their petty meanness and inhuman savagery. They are all around us, our fellow citizens in God's world, who turn into pedophiles, pathological killers, unscrupulous politicians, greedy corporate leaders, obnoxious neighbors, and family members who are a constant pain in the neck. Why does God give selfishness so much freedom? When will the badness warrant some attention from the giver of all perfect gifts (James 1:17)?

Many families know the trauma of seeing a child succumb slowly to leukemia, of having a strong, vibrantly-alive father and husband being so dreadfully ravaged by cancer that finally it's a mercy when death comes, of caring for a grandmother whose beautiful mind is totally disoriented by dementia.

The problems I have mentioned above have led thoughtful believers to wonder, "How can God be both good and almighty, when there is so much evil in the world?" The problem emerges out of the assumption that a good God would use his power to control or limit evil. However, many conclude that since the existence of evil cannot be denied then God cannot be both good and almighty. Many Christian thinkers have devised careful answers to the problem. This vindication of God has been labeled "theodicy." I will leave the theodicy issue now; thorough treatments can be found in many resources. Here I will ask the question, in view of the evil that every honest person can see, can we still hope for a good future?

Hope requires that we keep on trusting in God's providential oversight. But what we observe is that the caring action of God, if it is operative at all, is dispensed inconsistently, unpredictably and capriciously. So, how can we hope when we know that bad things, horrible, painful things, unbelievable things keep on happening in this human world? How can we think of the almighty God as our Father when there is very little evidence that his children receive any particular attention?

An honest examination of our problem must begin with the conviction that the God we worship is a God who acts. The Bible does not begin by describing the powers, virtues, characteristics, or traits of God. God is simply presented as the Creator; he makes stuff and enjoys it (Prov. 8:30, 31). The story of God and Israel is sprinkled with many anecdotes of how God responded to the dire straits of his chosen people and acted for them with astounding miracle power.

The Incarnation, the appearing of Israel's Jahweh in human flesh, revealed how God is – what are his qualities, his values, his attributes, and his attitudes to the evil powers that create havoc on earth. Jesus also demonstrated what kind of authority and power God has over the forces of darkness. Jesus was here to make God known (John 1:18). And, apparently, an important aspect of that demonstration was to move among people and do wonderful things for them.

Every miracle that Jesus did was a message from God. The miracles provided tangible witness to the fact that God is against illnesses, hunger, disabilities, demon oppression, and death. The miracles give us the clear and irrefutable impression that God cares. And that he has the authority and the power to deal with all human maladies and with the powers that afflict us. Jesus wasn't just showing off, like a circus illusionist. He wasn't out to impress; he had come to help. The miracles, or works of power as they are sometimes called (in John's Gospel they are called signs), were evidences of Jesus's Messianic integrity. They were expressions of God's compassion and they were promises of God's purpose for the human future.

The Gospels never give the impression that God is the cause of the leprosy, blindness, deafness, and demon affliction that Jesus encountered. Nor do they suggest that people deserved their troubles or that their sins called for a good dose of misery. Further, we don't get the impression that God is responsible to wipe it out. This was how the world was that Jesus visited. And the compassion of the Father and the Son moved them to offer their help.

The fundamental truth about the goodness of God that is celebrated in both Testaments seems to clash irreconcilably with the common realities of human life in this world. It is a fact that the most horrible tragedy may smash into the life of the most devoted Christian believer. It is frightening to realize that God seems to allow full freedom to all manner of evil. It is even more shocking to observe that evil *people* have the freedom to inflict atrocious abuses on their fellow humans. Doesn't God care?

The answers that Christian people give to the tragedies of life are usually trite, thoughtless, and even spiritually abusive. We've all heard the sanctimonious, "God must have a lesson for you in this dreadful pain," or, "At the end of the day you'll be a better person for it." And then there are the insinuations that the sufferer must be hiding some secret sin that God is punishing. The effort to be biblical may lead to, "But you know, all things work together for good," or "Your little girl is an angel now." The worst, in my view, is, "Well, after all we know that God is in control." I will respond to this misguided and misplaced unwisdom later in this chapter.

Some theologians point to the cross and suggest that seeing the Son of God, on his visit here from heaven, suffer an abominable death by crucifixion helps us understand the mystery. I'm not sure that it solves the problem; it just shows that God joined us in it. It seems to expand the confusion. What it does do, however, is show us that God joined us in our earthly dilemma and became vulnerable; he allowed himself to be abused and insulted with the most horrible death that humans have devised – crucifixion. As we watch Jesus on the cross we hear his lament, "My God, my God, why have you forsaken me?" We are shocked by the human authenticity of his degrading experience. There was nothing profound or dignified or God-like about that cross. Jesus felt as God-forsaken as any other human would feel in such a situation.

Further, the crucifixion of the Son shows us that God chose non-violent love as the means by which to redeem a world that was steeped in violence. God stared into the face of "the myth of redemptive violence" (Walter Wink's famous line) and chose to demonstrate a different redemptive approach. God chose not to respond in kind. The world operates on the principle that a kick deserves a good kick in return. God's providence works by an unworldly principle; it is the way of love.

\* \* \*

The common human mindset is that the experience of evil cannot be reconciled with the doctrine of a loving God. If God is love he should use his power to protect people, at least those who adhere to him and worship him. This assumption, that God has the power to protect us from harm, and fails at his duty if he doesn't, has been a common obstacle for Christian hope.

In the *Christianity Today* issue of July/August, 2018, Brittney Martin explores the problem I have been discussing here by reviewing what happened in Texas in 1987. A group of youth leaving a Bible camp after a week of studying and worshipping God was engulfed by the raging Guadalupe River on their trip out of the camp and ten young people perished. Now, thirty-one years after the fatal tragedy Martin called on some of the survivors and some of the bereaved family people. The early questions were still smoldering in their minds. What went wrong? What had they done wrong? Why do such terrors happen? Can one hope for any good at all, with a hope that is based on trust in a faithful God, in the face of such unanswerable questions? Where is our all-powerful God, the God of infinite love, when such soul-shattering horrors explode around us? How do we square the God of heaven with the life that we see on earth? One father declared even now, "God killed my daughter!"

Whatever we do with such burning questions or with such a searing, intractable pain, I agree with the convictions of Orthodox theologian David Bentley Hart. After the 2004 Indian Ocean tsunami that killed 230,000 people, he said, "Nothing that occurred that day or in the days that followed told us anything about the nature of finite existence of which we were not already entirely aware." We do not base our views of God on what we experience or see around us; rather, we try to interpret what happens in light of what we believe about God.

The explanations that have been thrown up by the defenders of theism to vindicate the apparent oversights of this loving God are many. Some theories say God allows suffering to make us better people. Others postulate that God allows evils into our lives to highlight the blessings that are also there. Some speculate that somehow we all have to contribute, by our suffering, to right the imbalance caused by all the rebellion and sin that God suffers from the world's people. Others reason darkly that God is so offended by universal human depravity, that the worst suffering is actually only a small taste of what we deserve.

Jamie Aten, Wheaton College psychologist, speaks of the "just world theory" that many people supposedly live by. It's the vain, unexamined concept that the world is fair. Bad people may run into badness but the good will pass through the fire unsinged, as did the three young men in the biblical story of Daniel. The theory may lead the victims of tragedy to believe they are being punished by the anger of God. Aten says we need a more biblical view that will allow us to worship the God of love in the worst extremities. Those who live by the "just world theory" may quickly become victims of "shattered assumptions." Brittany Martin suggests such shattered assumptions may contribute to the severity of post-traumatic stress syndrome (PTSD). The shattered assumption may lead to unbelief, to atheism, or to a shaky effort to maintain faith in a rather impotent, diminished God.

The dark mystery that we are exploring must have engulfed the first parents, Adam and Eve. One son, because of a minor resentment, turned against his younger brother and clubbed him to death. The Creator had informed them that their disobedience would bring a series of hardships into their life; life would be tough. Now, as the first parents ever to experience familial hatred, murder, death, and grief, they must have understood what their God had meant. And they must have wondered if God could not have done a better job of looking after their family. Could God not have controlled Cain's anger? The story was probably inserted here in the early narratives to provide us with a warning – this is what living in a sinful world may entail.

We need to take a careful look at the mistaken idea that God is in control. I have heard this opinion pronounced with pious conviction after all kinds of shocking disasters. It is used like a universal truism. It's trotted out rather thoughtlessly because it seems like the proper religious thing to say. "One thing we know for sure; God is in control." This simple saying is used to brush away any natural or man-caused disaster. Maybe we have learned the bad habit from the insurance companies. They label certain natural disasters as "acts of God." The term is used as a safeguard against insurance claims after disastrous events. The wording of their policies suggests God may do bad things. To distraught bereaved people this may indicate that God has killed their loved one by the lightning strike or the tornado.

The idea that God is in control may also develop out of the theological determinism that is taught in certain circles. The doctrine says that everything, the good and the bad, has been decreed by God before the creation of the world. In other words, God is the first cause of everything. For some people, this seems to say that God is to blame for everything. That is followed then by the pessimistic, fatalistic conclusion that since everything has already been determined "whatever will be will be."

The tentative solution I propose is that we must understand that God has given nature over to the rules by which it functions. God does not send flood waters our way and God does not stand in the gap to keep them away. But God is with us in every flood, whether physical or metaphorical. Can God not do miracles to save? Yes, the Bible affirms he can. But the Bible also witnesses just as clearly to the fact that sometimes he doesn't. Every flood or tornado or epidemic shows that God's protection seems to work very capriciously. Or, as I have sometimes wondered, when that thunderstorm swept over the golf course why did the lightening hit one golfer while a hundred went home unharmed? The issue is not just intellectual, although it has hounded many intellectuals almost to distraction. The problem is lived out at ground level over and over in disaster after disaster. Every person will at some point have to somehow reconcile their trust in God with the way life happens to them. And the better part of spiritual wisdom is not even to try to figure out *why* was this person saved and that one lost.

* * *

And now we finally face *our* question, "Where is the hope in all of this mysterious evil?" The first affirmation we must make is that the God who seems to be absent is actually present. The hope is that the God who seems to have abandoned us is participating with us in our horrors. We must trust that the God who seems powerless and impotent will with his non-violent love counteract and overcome the worst that the agents of evil throw at us. Maybe it helps to realize that any flare-up of evil, whether by nature, by evil people, or by the supernatural forces of darkness are, first of all, attacks on the good and gracious Creator. The evil that is dashed into our faces is also thrown insolently into the face of God.

One of my favorite theologians, N. T. Wright, says somewhere that the Scriptures seem far more interested in helping us cope with our sufferings than with helping us understand its causes or reasons.

The Bible records many bad things without trying to rationalize them. There was Job, completely confused by the accumulation of miseries he had to endure. We read the story now and we know about the spiritual conflict that went on behind the scenes; Job was not informed about that. He struggled fiercely with his dilemma. At the end he could relax, not because he understood the evil but because he now understood God.

The Hebrew singer who penned Psalm 73:1-14 wanted to praise God but was tormented with confusion when he saw that unrighteous people were wealthier and healthier than he was. However, at the end he receives the grace to confess, "But for me it is good to be near God." That new insight blessed him with peace.

The prophet Habakkuk was informed by the Lord that the Chaldeans (Babylonians) would attack and destroy Jerusalem. The good prophet was scandalized. What? Why, those Chaldeans were even more evil than his friends in Jerusalem. "Why do you look on the treacherous, and are silent when the wicked swallow those more righteous than they?" he screamed at God (1:13). God does not explain how his justice works but gently reminds the prophet that his righteous people (such as the prophet) have to live by faith (2:4). At the end the prophet's faith triumphs and he can announce that even if everything goes wrong, "Yet I will rejoice in the Lord; I will exult in the God of my salvation" (3:18). At this point I must add that I think it's normally and properly human to wrestle with the meaning of trouble and suffering. In fact, I dare say God expects us to be tormented by the unfairness of life.

In conclusion I suggest that the healthiest approach to the painful problems of earthly life is to focus on God's solidarity with us in our suffering. God has in his human state experienced it all himself – the abuse, the pain, the sense of abandonment, and even death. Further, we should remind ourselves that God is on the side of all those who reach out to their fellow sufferers with compassion and comfort. They are doing God's work. And then there is the long-range forecast – somehow at the end, all things will be well.

### For Further Thought and Study

*1. Review the three kinds of earthly troubles presented in the first three paragraphs and ask yourself, which of these is the most confusing? Why?*

*2. Look at the "words of comfort" that are often spoken to sufferers, as given above. What truth is there in each, but why should they never be used?*

*3. You've heard the quip, "God is an expert at making lemonade out of lemons." What is the wisdom in this saying and what seems wrong?*

*4. How do you respond to the author's argument that God does not intend to be in control?*

*5. Even though the freedom of nature and of human powers frightens us, why is this better than a world in which everything would be divinely regulated?*

*6. Review the experiences of the three Old Testament sufferers that the author mentions (for Job read 7:1-11) and ask yourself, "How would my faith handle such a painful dilemma?"*

# Chapter 5 – Hope and Prayer

*Prayer is not overcoming God's reluctance; it is laying hold of his highest willingness.* – Archbishop Richard Trench

*Hope alone is to be called realistic, because it alone takes seriously the possibilities with which all reality is fraught.* –Jurgen Moltmann

*What God wants to do for his people he moves them to ask him to do.* – Charles Spurgeon

*Take delight in the Lord, and he will give you the desires of your heart* (Psalm 37:4).

*And this is the boldness we have in him, that if we ask anything according to his will, he hears us (1 John 5:14).*

I begin with a basic, simple definition of prayer. Prayer is conversation with God. It is communication between us and God, silently or audibly, privately or as a group. It may consist of giving thanks, of praise, of asking for help, of confession, of seeking guidance, of interceding for others, or of listening. It is not the same as meditation or talking to ourselves *about* God. Meditation does not require an audience. Prayer does; it is talking *to* God. From a simple human perspective prayer is indeed rather odd. No God is visible; in fact, no God has ever been seen. But we believe he is listening. And we believe that our talking to God will in some way make a difference. We realize there may be millions of people, scattered all over the world, who are simultaneously addressing the same God, but we believe the one God pays attention to all these praying people. In fact, I suggest that if all seven billion of us would sincerely cry to God at the same time, God would hear every prayer and pay sincere attention to each. Sort of wonderful and weird, isn't it?

I began to write this book while reflecting on the question, how can we retrieve our hope when hoping looks hopeless? Our first recourse must be prayer. However, one would not pray unless there was already some hope at hand. Prayer doesn't make sense without hope; it would not continue without at least some hope. But hope in prayer is a fragile element because, as shown above, God's noticeable responses to our earthly needs are anything but predictable and consistent.

In this chapter, prayer means petition. It is approaching God for help. This is the kind of praying Jesus most often discusses in the Synoptic Gospels. Our prayers of petition may be beset by either of two problems. There is presumption, a premature, selfish, self-willed anticipation of what we expect to get from God. And then there is the opposite despair, the premature, pessimistic, arbitrary anticipation of non-fulfilment. "It won't do any good anyway!"

I wrote above about Jacques Ellul's discussion of God's current silence. It's as if God has gone into hiding. He says there is a real discrepancy between the eternal plan revealed in Christ Jesus and the concrete situation of the present time. However, we must hope in spite of the apparent silence because we *need* a God who listens to us and is ready to act. That we still hope in the silence is an indictment of God. We don't believe he is actually absent. We are unwilling to accept that God has no new word for us. And so, we protest and accuse God on the basis of his word. With a persistent and stubborn hope we challenge God to live up to his promises. As Ellul says, "So let God show that he actually is maintaining our right, that he is walking with us, that he is all around us and is going before us" (p. 181).

In our hopeful praying we refuse to accept the status quo. Not only do we refuse to accept God's silence, we refuse to put up with reality as it is. We take our stand with our silent God, we support God in his role of being the opposition (in parliamentary terminology), and speak out in his support. We stand with God against the powers of darkness. We join God in opposing injustice, ignorance, superstition, materialism, personal and corporate selfishness. In prayer we refuse to leave our earthly situation as is.

This means that in prayer we submit to the will of God. What we call prayer is not prayer unless it's spoken submissively. We can only pray if we agree with God and pray according to his will. However, submissiveness is not passive resignation. Resignation says nothing can be done, so let come what may. Hope is the opposite. We must persevere in prayer because we, our world, and our circumstances need to change; everything is out of whack. By ourselves we cannot fix it. We have to stand with God, plead with God, and expect God to do the changing. It seems like a mystery; the almighty God needs us to support him in his providential oversight of the world. Desmond Tutu once wrote, "For whatever reason, since humankind showed up on the scene, God does nothing without a human partner."

\* \* \*

To understand how God works on earth we must recall the incarnation of the eternal Son. When God wanted to act on earth he did not send out an angel brigade. He took on human form for himself and worked as a man among his fellow humans. In our wonder over the mystery of the incarnation we have forgotten that He works, not from above, but from within. As he once worked here through Jesus so he wants to work now through Jesus' people.

We must always remember that we are not on our own in our work, nor in our praying. We should not ever try to change God's mind. Prayer is not a tactic to change circumstances according to our wishes. It is not pestering an unwilling deity for a favor. Such thinking changes prayer into a pagan rite. If you merely want to have your own way there is no need to pray. Prayer would then be a waste of time, and an extremely frustrating way of wasting it. If you can't trust in God's higher knowledge you cannot pray. If you see prayer as a contest between you and God to see who has the strongest willpower, like a spiritual arm-wrestling match, you will lose out. That reminds me, sometimes Christians speak about wrestling with God in prayer. Such language is alright, provided that we understand that we are not wrestling to overpower God but to overcome our selfishness.

You may have wondered, what does God do when Christians pray against each other? That may happen when we beseech God about the weather, athletic contests, job applications, or market prices. Whose prayers will God honor. Abraham Lincoln pointed out during the

American Civil War that both sides believed in God and prayed for victory. He wondered, "What must God think of us?"

When God acted on earth in Jesus Christ he acted in self-sacrifice. He acted freely and he acted *in character.* What God did in Christ is at the very heart of the Divine identity. As we see Jesus stop for all kinds of people, listen to all kinds of needs, reach out with healing power to all, refuse the option of violence as he sought to inaugurate his new kingdom, submit to the decision that the Jewish defenders of the Jewish traditions had agreed upon, and then turn to the Father as he died on the cross and asked that his killers be forgiven, we gasp, "So that is the kind of God he is." And so, Gregory Boyd of Minneapolis keeps on reminding us in his writings, "If you want to know what God is like, look at Jesus."

In 1957, Harry Blamires, a British scholar wrote, "He is the kind of God whose nature is best expressed in his coming to earth and bringing salvation to men" (Blamires, p. 34). To this he adds, "Our Lord's earthly career, then, is the pattern of God's activity" (Blamires, p. 28). In 2015 Bradley Jersak of British Columbia published a more popular version of the same idea in *A More Christlike God.* He also argues that for us to understand the gospel correctly we must accept the idea that Jesus was here to reveal God to us. If we want to know what we can expect from God, look at what he kept on doing in the person of Jesus. Blamires suggests that if an intelligent Buddhist would carefully read the New Testament his first observation would be, not that God is love, nor that he sacrifices himself, but that this is a God who *does things.* That is why we pray. We are loyal disciples (I hope) of a God who is out to change the world, with its human residents, into its intended shape and form. We support his work in prayer, in the hope that God's vision will eventually come true.

God initiated, through Jesus, the changes that needed to happen on earth. When we pray in hope we are aligning ourselves and agreeing with God's will. We cannot change God's mind. In prayer we agree with God. In prayer we express our trust in the validity of his will. It would be heretical to try to change it. Rather, we try to understand it. The first step in learning what his will is all about is to notice what he did in the person of Jesus. Quickly we will learn that prayer is not pestering an unwilling deity for a personal favor. It is not a desperate attempt to convince God to do what we cannot do for ourselves. As Archbishop Trench understood it, prayer is not trying to overcome God's reluctance; it is trying to understand his will and then aligning ourselves with the will of God.

It is often said that we must have absolute and total confidence that we will get what we pray about. I heard a celebrated preacher declare that many Christians pray too much. They pray without having a clear conviction about God's will; such praying is a waste of time, he said. Even on this we should learn from Jesus. As he understood what would be the outcome of his commitment to teach the full truth of God – his critics would accuse him of blasphemy and condemn him to death – he prayed that he might be spared from such a fate. But even the Christ, in his human agony, apparently did not have clear insight into God's will. So, as he prayed for help he added, "Yet not what I want but what you want" (Matt. 26:39). Often I pray that way myself. It seems to me one can have strong faith in God, while still praying tentatively, as Jesus did.

Let me list here some of the more impressive promises about answered prayer that we have in John's writings. "If you abide in me, and my words abide in you, ask for whatever you wish, and it will be done for you" (John 15:7). Before you jump for joy and start your wish list, notice it starts with remaining in Jesus and letting his words remain in us. As we maintain close fellowship with Jesus and his word we will begin to wish as he wishes. We will value what he values, and we will then pray along with his desires.

"Very truly, I tell you, if you ask anything of the Father in my name, he will give it to you" (John 16:23). This does not refer to the glib "In Jesus' name, amen," with which we often sign off our praying. This requires that we understand Jesus mind so well that we can pray his prayers. We are to stand in for Jesus in our praying.

"And this is the boldness we have in him, that if we ask anything according to his will, he hears us" (1 John 5:14). This is empowering; this is tremendously encouraging. We don't need to be afraid of making mistakes in prayer. We will not damage God's people or God's programs by our praying. Our praying will never accomplish anything that would contradict God's will. Further, even though some of us have made some major and ruinous personal mistakes, we will never bring harm upon ourselves by praying about our needs. Harry Blamires says God loves us too much to give us, in answer to our praying, that which would merely feed our pride, our sense of superiority over others, or our spirit of self-sufficiency. It is safe to pray.

To sum up this teaching about prayer and the will of God I remind you of Mary, the young, unmarried woman in Nazareth. When the angel announced that she had been chosen to give birth to a holy son who would be known as "Son of God," she simply agreed, "Let it be with me according to your word" (Luke 1:38).

* * *

At this point some readers may wonder, why do we need to pray at all if we can only request what God wills? This is another of those great supernatural mysteries about which we wonder – and we should – but we must not allow it to ruin our faith or turn us from doing what is right. Some wise person once said, "Never allow that which you don't understand turn you away from what you do understand."

We understand that God visited this earth in the person of Jesus to establish a new people movement. The prophets of old foresaw it as a great, new kingdom. Jesus called it the Kingdom of God or the Kingdom of Heaven. The Kingdom is intended for all people; it is intended to bring all human conduct on earth into conformity with the values of heaven (Matt. 6:10). What Jesus began, he entrusted to his disciples. We understand that all of us current believers, wherever we are on earth, have inherited the disciples' assignment. We are to proclaim Jesus as Lord to all peoples, and we are to pray constantly and persistently that the kingdom will spread into every heart, every home, and every corner of this earth. This is our God-given task, whether we understand why we are needed for this or not.

Jesus spoke two parables to emphasize the need for stubborn, relentless, persistent prayer (Luke 11:5-8; 18:1-8). We are to be audacious enough to keep on praying even if it may seem that God hears nothing. This insistent challenge to God, that he is to act according to his word, is also an expression of confidence. In spite of the apparent silence we keep on praying and we hope to be heard. Hope saves us from bitterness, from resentful despair, or from giving in to disenchantment.

We do well to learn from Job of the Old Testament. Like him, we may find ourselves on the garbage dump of pathetic misery. Notice how he felt about God. Throughout his miserable laments (Chapters 3 – 31) he howls and screams at the injustice of God, but he never loses hold of God. The horrible physical misery, the abandonment of his family, the betrayal of his friends, the confused sermonizing of the four comforters, and the silence of God do not change his faith in God. Suddenly, in the midst of it all he breaks out in praise, "I know that my Redeemer lives, and that at the last he will stand upon the earth, and after my skin has been destroyed, then in my flesh I shall see God" (19:25-26).

From Job, the sheep farmer of antiquity, we turn to Jesus on the cross on the little hill near Jerusalem. Like Job, he also had no sins to confess. However, the ordeals of the night and the utter degradation of the cross led him to gasp, "My God, why have you forsaken me?" We may rationalize that it was not possible for God to leave the Son, and that the eternal Holy Trinity could not be split apart. We might rationalize that he knew better because he had announced that God would raise him from the dead. That's not abandonment! But all such quibbling does not change the reality of his experience; he felt alone, forsaken, rejected like the scum of the earth. That experience shows us how completely the incarnation integrated him into humankind. He felt as debased and demeaned as you or I would feel in such a situation. But he prayed to the God who was there and still listening to the pleading of the Son.

In that lament of Jesus we see the possibility that every person and every church may go through a similar sense of abandonment. If that was what Jesus had to go through for the saving of the world, why would that not sometimes be required of us? After reflecting on Job, and then on Jesus, why does it seem strange if sometimes our praying seems like a shout into the darkness. When Jesus prayed there was no answer from heaven; God was silent. The answer came three days later when Jesus, in his glory, walked out of the burial tomb. And then it came again with a blast fifty days later when the sound of the storm, the flames of fire, the foreign tongues, and the bold preaching of Peter resulted in three thousand people committing themselves in loyalty to Jesus. The Kingdom was on its way. These examples remind us to keep on waiting in prayer; who knows how many days our answers will be held in the waiting room of God's loving care before the answer will be granted?

When we pray about the future we assume the future is open and that God is free to act. We reject the idea of destiny and the premise that whatever will be, will be. In hope we reach out to the possibilities of the future with a vibrant expectation. In Christian prayer we search and grope for that which may seem naturally impossible and historically improbable. Heraclitus, the early Greek philosopher of change is supposed to have said, "He who does not hope for the unexpected will not find it."

Our God is the God of change. Throughout the Bible there is a contrast between the old and the new. The catchword that we must catch is "new." To the chagrin of all the ideological conservatives among us we must assert that our God is the God of the forward progress. Things are not intended to remain the same. The Old Testament has the exodus out of Egypt to the new homeland, then the return to new life in Judea after the years in Babylon, the new temple after the restoration, and the promise of the new lifestyle of peace when "the mountain of the Lord's house" will rise above all other mountains (Isa. 2:2-4). The New Testament speaks of the new covenant, the new commandment, the new heaven and the new earth, and then the new Jerusalem. The apostle reminds us that God "gives life to the dead and calls into existence the things that do not exist" (Rom. 4:17). Since we trust in a God who wants to bring new things into existence, to create what has never been, then even that which is not and which we cannot see or explain becomes thinkable because God's word gives us the authority to hope for it.

Our God is the God of promise. The promises of God form the unique basis for all Christian praying. God is revealed in the Old Testament as the Lord who looks after his people. He looks ahead into the future and predicts what he will do for them and through them. The New Testament is a continuum of the Old. He is still the God who is always present with his people. His people wait on him in hope and prayer, emboldened and encouraged by the Christ event. While the prophetic ministry of Jesus ended in a sordid death, it was, nevertheless, culminated with the glory of the resurrection. The God who guided Jesus throughout his earthly sojourn promises to bring us, with all of humankind, and even this physical earth, through to a glorious future. Eventually, the promise says, there will be a new heaven and a new earth in which all that is right will be at home (2 Peter 3:13).

Our God is the God of the future. Moltmann says God's "essential nature" is to be future-oriented. In early times God revealed himself to Moses as Jahweh (Ex. 3:13-15). That name can be interpreted as "I will be what I will be." God will be there in the future with his people. When God's people turn to him in prayer they are entrusting the future into his hands. Moltmann explains, "The hoped-for future is not only different because it is new but also because it is God's future. Still, this future does not, on the other hand, lie in the hand of blind fate or whimsical chance but rather in the power of this God who will create it (*Planning*, p. 183).

I move toward the conclusion of this chapter with the reminder that when we speak of fulfilled prayer we don't mean that there was a coincidental convergence of factors in our favor. One may fancy that it is a more mature view of life and reality to be able to dig up a natural explanation for the good thing that has blessed us. But the Scriptures teach us to thank God in everything (Eph. 5:20). We are to see God as having the freedom to respond to all our petitions. Yes, we may notice that the circumstances that favor us seem to be arranged coincidentally, but we see God's hand in that arrangement.

Nobody likes the thought of failing in prayer. We fear failure. The effort to defend oneself against disappointment may then lead a person to simply accept the present reality as it is. It is easy to fall into the worship of realism and expect no divine intervention. But Moltmann warns, "In adopting this so-called realism dictated by the facts we fall victim to the worst of all utopias – the utopia of the *status quo*" (*Theology of Hope*, p. 23). He adds, "God has exalted man and given him a life that is wide and free, but man hangs back and lets himself down" (p. 22). So, I trust the Holy Scriptures, I agree with the insights of Jurgen Moltmann, but I also accept the realities of this life.

All this results in a dilemma, which I now illustrate with my recollection of a young man I once visited; he was in his late twenties and extremely sick with cancer. He told me he had friends who kept on rebuking him for his lack of faith. If he would only believe in healing, God would heal, they preached at him. But he was afraid, he said, to base his whole hope on a miracle healing. If the healing would *not* happen he might lose his faith and that would be worse than anything. I tried to explain carefully that one can believe fully in God's *ability* to heal but recognize realistically that at some point or another God let's all humans die. God's ultimate purpose for us is not endless health in this era, but ultimately to be with him in eternal glory. And in that eternal, spiritual dimension there will be perfect health. So, keep on trusting and praying,

I advised; he would either be healed now or go home to the healthy life of eternity. Suddenly his eyes lit up with the joy of a new comprehension, and he sank back into his pillows in peace. Two weeks later he moved over to the new home where he would never suffer again (2 Cor. 5:4).

## For Further Thought and Study

*1. After reading this chapter how do you feel about Moltmann's view (top of the chapter) that hope alone is realistic. How do you keep your hope from becoming unrealistic wishfulness?*

*2. Consider the author's distinction between submissiveness and resignation. How do you cope with the occasional urge to "throw in the towel" and just resign yourself to whatever may happen?*

*3. Consider Desmond Tutu's saying that God needs us as his partners. The author says that, first of all, partnership calls us to pray. Why does God need our praying?*

*4. Here are a few samples of the unrestricted promises the Bible has about God's providential care: Psalm 84:11; 34:10; Matthew 6:33; Philippians 4:19. How does this agree with what we see happening to God's people today?*

*5. The author stresses that our praying must agree with God's will. How does one understand, and get a feel, for the will of God?*

*6. Read what Jesus said about answers to prayer: Matthew 7:7-11; 18:19; Mark 11:24; 9:23. Why is there so little coherence between these unqualified promises and the results of our praying?*

# Chapter 6 – Hope for Revival

*The Christian hopes for two things: . . . hope for a new creation, and hope for the just reign of God in this present creation.* – Nicholas Wolterstorff

*Imagine social movements rising out of spiritual revival and actually changing the wind of both our culture and our politics.* – Jim Wallis

*What is needed to move our culture into some measure of conformity to God's will is God-centered and kingdom-centered thinking.* – Richard F. Lovelace

*Do not be conformed to this world, but be transformed by the renewing of your minds* (Rom. 12:2).

*You were taught . . . to be renewed in the spirit of your minds, and to clothe yourselves with the new self, created according to the likeness of God* (Eph. 4:22-24).

God's voice calls out to us from deep within the last book of Holy Scripture, "Behold, I am making all things new" (Rev. 21:5). This word of promise gives us the freedom to expect the renewal of all that lives. Let's imagine this means that when our religious institutions get frozen up in the ice of ancient traditions, or when our personal lives get so dry and dusty that we seem to be prematurely ready for the grave, God can move upon us with his invigorating grace and infuse our being with new life. I invite you to think about it. In this current chapter I will focus specifically on the prospects and the problems of corporate Christian revival. Can our churches and denominational structures and para-church agencies be revived to new vigor when it looks as if they are headed toward an imminent death?

The term "revival" has been used for centuries of a new appreciation for the faith of the past. Church historians have chronicled many such movements in the English world during the 18th and the 19th centuries.

The Puritan minister Cotton Mather spoke in 1702 of a "general religious *awakening* in a community." The more common contemporary term with the same sense is "renewal".

The entire history of Israel was marked by a series of declines and renewals in their loyalty to Jahweh. The narratives of Judges reveal an age when "all the people did what was right in their own eyes" (17:6, 21:25). But God did not turn away from his faltering people. There were frequent times of renewal, usually initiated by strong leaders who emerged to call their people to destroy their idols and reaffirm their loyalty to their traditional Lord. Then they led them in victorious battle against the latest foreign invaders.

These cycles of decadence and subsequent renewal continued throughout the later history of Judah. The most significant revival was guided by young king Josiah, who took over a nation that his grandfather Manesseh had led into utter depravity. Under his reign they treated the book of their law with new respect, the places of idol worship were systematically destroyed, and the worship of the Lord was reinstated in Jerusalem. The future suddenly looked much brighter for Judah (2 Kings 22, 23). His spiritual successes emboldened him (I suggest) and he led his army against the Pharaoh of Egypt. He was killed, at thirty-nine years of age. And his reforms died with him. Food for sobering thought!

Continuing now with the theme of renewal in our time, I suggest renewal has sometimes been seen mainly as a matter of finding new joy, new enthusiasm, new vigor and zest for the Christian life. The charismatic revival of the 20th century has blessed us with this emphasis. To that aspect of renewal I want to add the need to become renewed in obedience and to become passionate about following Christ in all aspects of personal and social living.

It seems ironical, does it not? The original sin, back in the first garden, was the vain attempt to believe the tempter and try to become like God. Now the most persistent human temptation is to suspect that humankind is in an inevitable downward spiral that drags us relentlessly deeper into the abyss of nihilism. Trying to be like God has been a failure. Is there now nothing left but to accept the current status quo and resign ourselves to the lethargy and inertia of despair? The issue faced me starkly in an e-mail letter from a fellow minister, commenting on my pastoral role as leader of an older church, "Since history shows that old churches eventually die and disappear there is not much for you to do but to preside over your church's demise." Ooh! I didn't like that. I still don't.

Praying in hope is always complicated by the unpredictable nature of the future. As the apostle once said when he was discussing our ministry in this world; the time of full knowledge is in the future, but now we "know only in part" (1 Cor. 13:12). This tends to diffuse our confidence. Because of our limited foreknowledge it would be easier to simply resign oneself to whatever may come than to pray with a specific future target in mind.

It is important for us to understand the dynamics of the kingdom of God. With the coming of Jesus God introduced a new system into the vortex of human cultures. It was a new people movement. It was not imposed upon people from on top. It was inserted here within our world by the visitor from heaven. When he returned to the eternal, spiritual dimension (the Bible calls it "heaven") he left here a nucleus of disciples-in-training who would now spread the kingdom message throughout the world. God's plan was, and still is, that the kingdom would be a world movement. It began in Palestine with Jesus, but it was for the world. The plan was that it would infiltrate and transform the many different cultural expressions of humankind with the values of heaven. You've probably prayed that it would happen. "May your will be done on earth as it is in heaven," is what you say when you pray the Lord's Prayer. That is why this new movement can also be called the "kingdom of heaven," as it is in Matthew's Gospel. At the heart of this heavenly outreach to the nations of the world is the stunning proclamation that Jesus is the Lord.

Before Jesus left he explained that his absence would be filled by the presence of the Holy Spirit. The invisible Spirit would guide the team of disciples as they would proclaim the good news of Jesus. The Spirit would also move in the hearts of the listeners and transform them into Jesus people. As we read the historical story of this world transformation we notice that it has been an irregular, unpredictable process. Some changes happened already in the days of the first disciples, some happened only much later. Sometimes changes occurred through the efforts of visionary human leaders. At other times it seems that the Spirit of God was advancing kingdom values even when the people of God were unaware of what was going on.

*  *  *

I illustrate the comments above with some material adapted from an earlier book of mine (*The Biblical Case for Equality*). There I showed how the vision of Galatians 3:28 has slowly worked its way into the fabric of human cultures. The vision, as stated by the apostle, is that in Jesus Christ the divisive distinctions between Jews and Greeks, between slaves and free people, between males and females would be replaced by a new sense of oneness. In a sense this seems like a minor adjustment of social values. However, it has had immense implications for how society is structured.

The first of the three divisions listed in Galatians 3:28 receives the most urgent attention in the Scriptures. It seems that, to begin with, even Jesus' disciples did not understand God's will on this issue. When Jesus said that they would be His witnesses to the ends of the world they apparently thought of this only as sharing Christ with Jewish people everywhere. The first major breakthrough in this restricted thinking came when Peter changed his mind. He received a definite divine message that he was to preach in the house of Cornelius, a Roman officer. When he did so the entire household of the Roman was awakened to the faith and received baptism. Later, when he explained the specifics of the divine call and the results of his obedience to his critical colleagues in Jerusalem, they exclaimed, "Then God has given even to Gentiles the repentance that leads to life" (Acts 11:18).

That burst of insight, however, did not solve all problems; in fact, it immediately created new difficulties for the church. If Jews and Gentiles could both be called Christians and belong to the same church, by whose moral principles would they live? That question necessitated the first major gathering of church leaders, as it is described in Acts 15. After an extensive consultation they agreed that, even though the church had begun with Jewish believers, the Gentiles who were now receiving Christ did not need to become Jews to be one with them. They received a new vision of the direction in which God was leading his church and they attributed this insight to the guidance of the Spirit (Acts 15:28). The council in Jerusalem was moved by the Spirit to recognize that unless the Jewish and the Gentile believers could accept each other as equals and live together in Christ, the church could not truly represent God's reconciling work. Racial segregation would be a denial of the gospel.

Compelling the Gentile to become a Jew would be a contradiction of God's way of redemption.

It remained for Paul, in his later letter to the Ephesians, to develop a systematic statement of the unity created by the sacrifice of Christ (2:11-22). He explains that the Jews who used to think of themselves as close to God, and the Gentiles who seemed to be far away, have now been brought together by Christ. The dividing wall has been broken down. In Jesus Christ there is peace between the people who were formerly separated. Through Christ God has now created one new humanity. Those who once were strangers and aliens are now fellow citizens. Consequently, there is only one church being built upon the one foundation. As a result of this unifying work of Christ they are now called upon to maintain and to live in the unity they already have in the Spirit (4:3). Spiritual unity is not only a theory; it is meant to be lived out in the church. And this unity of the races in the church is to show how the different races are to live together, with respect and harmony, in the world.

It is obvious that of the three sets of polarities mentioned in Galatians 3:28, the second and the third do not receive as much direct attention in the Scriptures as does the first. Apparently, the division between Jews and Gentiles, which existed primarily in the minds of the Jews, was so fundamentally contrary to the essence of what it means to be the church that no effort was spared to correct it. It should be remembered here that the Jewish concept of superiority and exclusiveness came out of God's dealings with them in the past. They thought they had been divinely chosen to be first among the peoples of the world. They had been called to be God's people; the Gentile nations had not received that same call. They could have argued that, if they were prejudiced, their prejudice was based upon God's election. The word of the Lord had always come to them through Hebrew speakers and in Hebrew words.

Similar arguments have been presented by those who have wished to defend the other two divisions that Paul mentions. It is not that long ago that some white believers devoutly believed that they had been designated, by creation, to have a superior role over blacks in society. And today many Christians still scour the Bible for arguments to bolster their feeling that women should be subordinate to men. Once a custom or a tradition is entrenched in society it cannot easily be vanquished.

However, in the first century the apostles of grace and freedom won their case. The Spirit was victorious. Gentile and Jewish believers could belong to one church. The traditions were superseded and the church kept on spreading out as one body.

The societal division, between slaves and free people, gets a different treatment than the first. Apparently, slave and master could function side by side in the same church (Col. 3:22-24; 1 Tim. 6:1-3; Philemon 16). No New Testament writers directly challenge the established convention of slavery in the Roman Empire. However, they teach both, slaves and masters, to respect each other as fellow Christians and to treat each other with Christian grace. This does not mean that it is right, or that it ever has been right, for one person to own another as personal property. Even though the principle of human equality was clearly declared in Galatians, Ephesians, and Colossians it was only in the nineteenth century that Western Christians could finally get themselves to face the social implications of this doctrine. Old traditions die hard.

Most Christians today are deeply distressed by the frequent reports of slavery and abuse of minority rights in different countries. They understand now that any discrimination on the basis of rank, ethnicity, or color is an affront to human dignity and a violation of the plan of the Creator. That European and North American governments frequently express concern over violation of human rights in other nations may often sound rather paternalistic, but it is still evidence of how extensively New Testament values have permeated even secular thinking.

The polarity between men and women is treated likewise, not with any ambivalence, but with patience. The principle of equality in Christ is emphatically pronounced, but the practical outworking of that, it seems, was left to time. Slavery would naturally become intolerable once masters and slaves would regard each other as fellow Christians – it still surprises me that it took so long. (In fact, we in our developed countries need to confess that the ideal of human equality is not yet being applied very consistently, right at home, in our relationships with the minority groups who live in our midst.) The polarity between men and women, on the other hand, would be erased once people would recognize that both male and female were created in the image of God and recall that at Pentecost women and men alike were filled with the Spirit and spoke out the good news of God's truth. And again, I am surprised that it has taken till recent times for the implications of creation and Pentecost to start sinking in.

* * *

To the discussion above I now add the observation that the Spirit's transforming work has sometimes begun outside of the church. Some examples: In the case of slavery, male/female relationships, and nonviolent international relationships, some secular leaders have put the church to shame. God has been able to enlighten secular leaders with new perspectives that seemed threatening to the church. They seemed too new. The church tends to think that the traditions of the past are holy. Leadership people, whether social, political, or religious, usually have a deep investment in maintaining the status quo. There is security in static stability. However, there have been notable changes in the past, as the Spirit has moved in the secular world and in the church. This should inspire us today with the hope that even now there may be a way toward a more God-like society in the future.

I will eventually speak about the scorn that many people of the world have for the concept of an eternal future. Here I now discuss the error of those Christians who are so focused on the future that they view the present with contempt. I have sometimes accused evangelicals of being addicted to bad news. They seem to think God's specialty is the future, not this current era. Many see no hope for the world of this time. They do not pray for revival and they do not work to induce it; they just listen for "the sound of the trumpet" (that would be the trumpet of 1 Thess. 4:16). They cannot take ecological concerns seriously, they see no value in helping the plight of the world's impoverished, and they are unconcerned about the plague of violence that has made some countries almost uninhabitable. The worst it gets the nearer is the coming of the Lord, is the watchword they live by.

One aspect of Christian theology that has made it difficult for some believers to be enthusiastic about renewal in the church and the expansion of the kingdom of God has been called "evacuation theology." The idea is that there is no hope for the world, and for the church. The only hope is for God to rapture (evacuate) his people quickly before it gets worse and then melt the whole thing down in a global holocaust of fire. You will notice in the following pages that I don't think the Bible predicts such a destiny. The future that I see in the Bible is not the removal of the church but the return of the church to a new heaven and a new earth (Rev. 21:1-10).

Now here is an alternative perspective: rather than giving up with this present civilization and the current church let us take heart from the fact that there have been many dark eras in the history of the world that have been followed by awakening and renewal. Further, we should understand that a warm concern to see the knowledge of God and the obedience of God develop among all peoples of the world does not distract from the ultimate hope of an eternal life in the new and glorified dimension of the future.

I do not deny the signs of cultural degradation and of a dying church that some observers decry. I see them too. But we cannot know if the current darkness is a sign of the coming of the Lord or the prelude to another worldwide renaissance ("renaissance" is the French word for rebirth). And anyway, the best way to prepare for the coming of the future world is to pray and work with all our hearts for the renewal of *this* world. The Irish/American scholar Os Guiness challenges his readers to "trust in God and his gospel and move out confidently into the world, living and working for a new Christian renaissance, and thus challenge the darkness with the hope of the Christian faith, believing in an outcome that lies beyond the horizon of all we can see and accomplish today" (*Renaissance*, p. 28). This noble challenge must be countered by the reminder that it is not up to us to save the world. Managing the world is best left to God. Our task is to walk with Jesus and bring the aroma of our Lord into all of our activities and into each of our relationships. Of course, we cannot know how our lives, endeavors, and prayers will affect the big picture. Our duty is to be faithful with what God gives us where God places us. Guinness describes our Christian role in this world thus:

> Whether our prospects as Christians today look bright or dismal, whether the tide of modern culture is flowing our way or against us, whether we are strong in numbers or almost seem to be on our own, such external factors are irrelevant. We must each follow our calling, pursue our utmost for his highest in every possible way and count unquestionably on the dynamics of the kingdom of God, and then, knowing our chronic ignorance and the probable incompleteness of our endeavors, trust the outcome to God (Guinness, p. 112).

Some of our Christian scholars tell us our task is "culture building." It's a noble thought, but the church's past experiences with remaking culture don't look encouraging. When the Emperor Constantine legitimized Christianity in 313 the church embraced its new freedom with enthusiasm and became active in the Empire. It didn't take long before the church was more like Rome than like Jesus. In Medieval Europe the bishops and popes enjoyed the power they shared with the secular rulers. In the process they became so secularized that when common people tried to go back to the Bible and live like Jesus they were seen as seditious traitors, branded as disloyal to the state, and suppressed with murderous ferocity. As Kierkegaard once explained, when everybody becomes Christian than Christianity is effectively abolished.

On the other hand, some of the nonconformists that came out of that era tried to separate totally from the world and build their own Christian culture. I'm thinking of the Hutterites, the Amish, and some of my conservative Mennonite friends. My observation is that the passion to create a pure and holy church may become such a legalistic quagmire that Jesus is lost in the mud. And such communities may become so self-absorbed that all thoughts of being a witness for Christ are lost as well. "Christian" cultures are always flawed.

One reason why the current church of Christ has been ineffective in its transformative ministry is that it has become too much like the world. The Pauline counsel that I quoted above, that we are to be renewed in our minds, is preceded by the crisp advice, "Do not be conformed to the world" (Rom. 12:2). Carl Henry's famous comment on this worldliness was, "Earlier it was next to impossible to get Evangelicals out into the culture. Now it is equally impossible to get the culture out of Evangelicals" (Guinness, p. 120). When King David realized his heart had become befouled by worldly culture, he prayed:

> Create in me a clean heart, O God,
> And put a new and right spirit within me.
> Do not cast me away from your presence,
> And do not take your holy spirit from me.
> Restore to me the joy of your salvation,
> And sustain in me a willing spirit.
>
> Then will I teach transgressors your ways,
> And sinners will return to you (Psalm 51:10-13).

The first six lines of this prayer can be seen as a recipe for personal renewal. Once he has received from God the gifts of a clean heart, a new spirit, and a refreshed joy the king will be able to speak to his ungodly neighbors about their sins and then they will listen. This theme of hope for *personal* renewal and restoration will be continued in the next chapter.

### For Further Thought and Study

*1. How does the current world scene affect you, with a sense of dark despair or with enthusiasm for the future? What depresses you and what excites you?*

*2. If you agree with the author that renewal is essentially God's work, in what way is our human involvement required?*

*3. In what ways do you think should your church or Christian circle pray for and expect renewal?*

*4. Read the account in Ezekiel 37 about the awakening of the dead bones (a figurative picture of the restoration of Judaism to their promised land) and ask, "What does this promise mean for the church of today?"*

*5. Read one of the Bible's most comprehensive calls to the new life, Colossians 3:12-17, and ask yourself, "How could such a life be realized in our churches today?"*

*6. Reflect on the meaning of the first six lines of King David's prayer and ask yourself, which of these needs should I personally bring to the Lord right now?*

# Chapter 7. Hope for the Human Sin Problem

*Jesus Christ, by His victory, broke the power of the forces of evil, and by His help that same victory can be ours.* – William Barclay

*Sins are so remitted, as if they had never been committed.* – Thomas Adams

*The blood of Christ covers all of our sins, but each of us must do personal business with God in order to experience his forgiveness.* – Lewis B. Smedes

*For I know my transgressions, and my sin is ever before me. Against you, you alone, have I sinned, and done what is evil in your sight* (Psalm 51:3, 4).

*Then I acknowledged my sin to you, and I did not hide my iniquity; I said, "I will confess my transgressions to the Lord," and you forgave the guilt of my sin* (Psalm 32:5).

To begin this chapter, I use the quaint comment that George Macdonald uses to conclude his discussion of the human problem, "Is it not the very essence of the Christian hope, that we shall be changed from much bad to all good?" (MacDonald, p. 51).

All of us, the human residents of this world, have a common problem. It is sin. We fall short of fulfilling the role for which God created us. In one way, or in many ways, we have all transgressed the design for human living that the Creator has for us. We are all walking in the steps of our first parents, who were also the first sinners, Adam and Eve. The Bible pictures sin as a form of bondage. Sin ties us up and leaves us as helpless slaves in the grips of a tyrannical master whose evil wishes direct our actions and from whose control we cannot free ourselves.

However, the great Creator God, the source of all love, who never acts without love, has embarked on a mighty project to redeem the world from its entrenched sin. The eternal Son has been here to set us free from the sin with which we condemn ourselves. It is a beautiful and wonderful thing and will result in glory. Let's explore this hope.

In the Christianity that I know there is far more emphasis on the blessing of being forgiven *for* our sinning than there is on the blessing of being set free *from* sinning. Rarely is freedom from sin preached as the first need of the human sinner. In some circles where I have worked and worshipped it was not even regarded as the true gospel to emphasize freedom from the life of sin; instead it was dismissed as preaching the works of the law. This is odd, it is unbiblical, it looks past the primary purpose of God's work on earth and focusses on the secondary as if that is the only thing about which God is concerned.

Writing out of a religious culture that is very different than mine, the English novelist Graham Greene, who is Roman Catholic, explores the painful dynamics of our problem in *The Heart of the Matter*. He pictures a lonely British military officer at his post in West Africa who has a lustful love for a young single woman in his town. After each sexual event he visits the local priest, confesses his sin, and receives absolution. Eventually the officer feels so defeated by his ongoing cycle of sin and remorse that he cries out to the priest, "Can't you somehow help me out of this lust problem?" The priest simply assures him that he will be there to grant him the sacrament of remission again the next time he needs forgiveness. In utter frustration the officer walks away and kills himself.

The radical reformers of the 16th century spoke to the same issue when they accused Martin Luther of creating a problem with his oft quoted maxim, "*simul justus et peccator*" (righteous and a sinner at the same time). It was probably misunderstood by the Anabaptists, who criticized him hotly. Luther meant to offer some pastoral comfort to those who had reached out to God in a justifying faith but were still troubled by continuing temptations and sinful habits. Anyway, it looked to the critics as if Luther's theology had created a nation of forgiven believers who still lived like pagans. The Anabaptists thought Luther's doctrine of justification by faith *alone* was causing a lifeless and sterile faith. Lutherans saw the Anabaptist emphasis on costly discipleship as a return to the works-righteousness and legalism of the Roman church. Some descendants of the Reformation can now see that the two are not really in conflict but are complementary parts of a full-orbed New Testament Christianity.

Before I move into the message of the New Testament, I use some insights from the saintly Scottish minister of over a century ago, George MacDonald. He is regarded as a pioneering figure in the field of fantasy literature. It seems to me that his fascination with the fantastical may have led him out of the bounds of orthodoxy but then it allowed him to see some aspects of true truth that others had overlooked. He complains that people want to be released from the consequences of their sins while they keep on living *in* those sins. He says first we need to be delivered from the indwelling badness that produces bad actions (p. 16). Humans, in the selfish hell of their disobedient hearts, want peace and happiness. The Lord knows what they *need*; they only know what they *want*. They want ease; God knows they need purity. To be saved only from the consequences of the badness – that is, to be forgiven only – would be an incomplete salvation. He agrees fully with the Scriptures when he concludes, "The Son has come from the Father to set the children free from their sins" (p. 20).

The New Testament begins its message of hope for human sinners by reporting that when the young prophet John appeared out of the bush to preach by the Jordan River, he attacked the sinfulness of his fellow Jewish people head-on. "You brood of vipers! Who warned you to flee from the wrath to come?" He warned that the axe of God's judgment was ready to chop down any trees that were not bearing good fruit (Luke 3:7-9). He invited his listeners to repent of their sins and receive baptism. The meaning of repentance (*metanoia*) is not merely regret over sin but a change of mind and a turning away from sins. Then when Jesus showed up on the river bank he cried out, "Here is the Lamb of God who takes away the sin of the world!" (John 1:29). Notice that! Jesus came to remove sin.

Here is a list of points at which Jesus confirmed that same concern for the problem of sin: "I have come to call not the righteous but the sinners" (Mat. 9:13). "There is joy in the presence of the angels of God over one sinner who repents" (Luke 15:10). "Light has come into the world, and people loved darkness rather than light because their deeds were evil" (John3:19). "You will die in your sins unless you believe that

I am he" (John 8:24). "But now that you say, 'We see,' your sin remains" (John 9:41).

The most detailed interpretation of the nature of our sin problem is given by the apostle Paul in Romans 6. His metaphorical language sees sin as a mean tyrant who enslaves us and forces us into a life of disobedience (v. 6, 12). When we unite ourselves by faith with the crucified Jesus we die to the sin that has enslaved us and are set free (v. 6, 7, 17, 18). Consequently, we are now free to align ourselves with the resurrected Jesus and live a new life (v. 5). There is no mention of guilt or forgiveness in the chapter. Paul's theme is repeated by Peter in slightly different terms, "For Christ also suffered for sins once for all, the righteous for the unrighteous, in order to bring you to God" (1 Peter 3:18). And then John explains how freedom from sin may be experienced. "If we confess our sins, he who is faithful and just will forgive us our sins and cleanse us from all unrighteousness" (1 John 1:9). Many people who comfort themselves with the first part of the promise don't pay attention to the second part. When we admit our sins (unrighteousness), not only will we be forgiven but the sins will be removed from us. That promise is reinforced in 1 John 3:5, "You know that he was revealed to take away sins."

To these references about the divine concern over human sin I add two reminders that Jesus came to *bear* the sins of the people (Heb. 9:28, 1 Peter 2:24). I have usually heard these verses interpreted as if all the sins of the world were placed upon Jesus on the cross so that he would be seen as guilty of it all. Some theologians even say that the wrath of God settled there upon Jesus because he was the worst of all sinners. Others say that since God cannot look upon sin, the Father abandoned Jesus on the cross. These creative theological accretions to the biblical witness ignore the basic meaning of the two verses used. In both of the texts I cited here the Greek word for bearing is *anaphero*. The verb does not suggest that sin was placed upon Jesus, but that Jesus picked up human sin and carried it away. This imagery coincides well with the statements above about Jesus taking away sin. If we need a biblical precedent for such an image we could look at the prescription for the ancient Day of Atonement. That ancient ritual concluded with the unclean skin, offal, and dung of the sacrificial animals being carried away, out of the encampment, and then burned with fire (Lev. 16:27).

You will notice that none of the Scriptures I have used above speaks about guilt. My concern, as a student of the Bible, is that many of my colleagues are so obsessed with the problem of guilt that they overlook the basic purpose of Christ's mission to earth. He came to create a new community of purified and holy people who would move out into the world and build the kingdom of God, both by their exemplary living and by their verbal witness. At this point I recall N. T. Wright's recent study *The Day the Revolution Began*. The "day" is the day Jesus died on the cross. Professor Wright argues that Jesus did not die so we could go to heaven (Actually, I'm sure he would agree that Jesus wants us with him in heaven). Wright emphasizes that Jesus died to save us from sinful living so we could live for the glory of God on earth. I think my paragraphs above point in the same direction. Anyway, now we are ready to move on to part two of the great hope that we sinful people can enjoy.

✳ ✳ ✳

First of all, the biblical catalogue of moral requirements is staggering in its scope. It's helpful to realize that the first part (we call it the Old Testament) is specifically designed for the people of Israel and their responsibilities under the covenant that Jahweh had made with them. Sincere Jews found the demands overwhelming (Rom. 7:7-13). Moving on from there, we find enough in Jesus' teachings about kingdom living to make us shudder with apprehension too.

In the course of his teaching Jesus reaches back into the Old Testament and sums up its ethical message with the big rule, "You shall love the Lord your God with all your heart, with all your soul, and with all your mind." Then he adds the second, which is just as important, "You shall love your neighbor as yourself" (Matt. 22:37-39). This, Jesus explains, sums up everything. Every sin we've ever committed is in some way a violation of these two divine laws. With these two commandments Jesus accuses all of us of being wrong and having done wrong. The apostle Paul would later sum it up climactically, "All have sinned and come short of the glory of God" (Rom. 3:23). Bad news!

Some find fault with God for this human dilemma; if his laws were not so strict it would be easier to live without sin and guilt, they say. To this we must explain that the laws of God were not arbitrarily formed out of thin air. The laws of God simply came out of the heart of God; they reveal, they show us, the nature of God. As Miroslav Volf has it, "Moral law is an expression of God's very being" (Volf, p. 143). Further, the laws of God were designed to make life in the human community as rich and peaceful as possible; in other words, God's laws are good for us. All of God's laws for people come out of a heart full of deep love for people.

In response to our moral failures the Bible, in both Testaments, repeats over and over the promise of forgiveness. God created a people who had the freedom to do either right or wrong and placed them in a world that would constantly entice them to use that freedom in the wrong way. The result is that human history has been tarnished with sin from beginning to end. Did God know how it would turn out? We think he did. But he dared to create people with the power to make their own choices because he is at heart a forgiver. Miroslav Volf, who ties together God's two great acts of mercy, the giving and the forgiving, sums it up well, "In view of the fact that before creating the world God knew that humans would sin, the God who gives by creating was from the start also the God who forgives" (p. 141).

A notice was posted on some factory bulletin board, "To err is human, to forgive is not company policy." I'm glad I work for a company that has a different policy. The manager of my company, "the kingdom of God," is willing and eager to forgive. In his gracious compassion he *offers* his forgiveness. In his kingdom we have all done wrong, but we are a company of forgiven servants.

Has it ever dawned on you that time is absolutely and relentlessly unforgiving? When something is done it's done. Whether it's good or bad, whether you're proud of it or ashamed of it, it stays done. Someone said, "The wheels of Time's chariots have ratchets on them; they turn only forward." Those with a mechanical bent to their thinking will understand this. You can never go back and live an event all over again to improve on it; the ratchet lets you only move forward. This simple fact provides endless opportunities for morbid reflection and despair.

The agony of guilt is pictured in Psalm 38:3-8 as a horrible case of bad health. The writer is sick, and the sickness is the memory of his past sin. He has a guilt problem, so bad that it's throttling the life out of him. You have heard the media speak of crime as pathological; there are pathological criminals. This Psalm speaks of guilt as pathological, as a dreadful, debilitating disease.

We start life with no experience that might teach us how or when to be careful. We have no school that will teach us how to live; we just start living. The problem is that to a greater or lesser degree we are all impulsive, we often act thoughtlessly. But there's a worse handicap we have; we all have a deep streak of perversity, some have called it "original sin," that resists the rules under which we are supposed to live. Sometimes this contrary spirit even *delights* in being bad and destructive. So, we all have ample opportunities for spoiling our own lives and soiling our own memories. Consequently, remorse or regret over the past is one of the most common of human emotions.

Some sinners can drown out the past, by frenetic busyness, by indulging in distracting pleasures, by drugging the senses with narcotics, or by planning even bigger and more daring iniquities. But those who have the courage to pause and review their past usually recall many failures. It's no fun. The guilty memory of the past can suffocate us with its controlling bondage.

Some sins can be made right. One can make sincere apologies to the offended one. The shop-lifted goods can be returned; or one can offer to pay. Restitution is possible. However, this does not erase the memory; even after there has been confession and restitution the sin or the crime continues to reside in one's memory.

Some of the most troubling remorse occurs over sins about which one is not sure. I've heard a person say, "I wish I knew if that was my fault or not. Then at least I would know what I am responsible for." You probably remember such questions yourself. Was I honest when I sold my old car, or did I cover up too much? Was that marriage breakup my fault, or his? Was it right to spank my children when they were young or did I sin against them?

The Bible is an insistent guilt-producer, as I explained above. It is so demanding that many prefer not to read it. Over and over the Scriptures hold before us God's demands for moral righteousness. Now, one can have a problem with a subjective, contrived, false guilt. This is a personal mental health problem. It is not the result of sinning but of a personal sense of inferiority. People can fabricate their own guilt by reflecting too much on their own inadequacy. However, the Bible repeatedly emphasizes the reality and objectivity of guilt. True guilt is real. It is real because God holds us responsible for our sinning. By the way, the King James Version of the Bible that I once used only twice uses the word "guilt." Otherwise, it repeatedly uses a term that is even more crushingly painful, "condemnation." Whatever terms are used to describe it, it's bad news indeed. However, the Bible also has a breath-taking message of promise – the incredible offer of complete deliverance from guilt and condemnation.

There is the good news of what God has already done to rescue us. Jesus has been here! The New Testament understands him as the physical presence of the mysterious, infinite, eternal God of Israel. He was the God of the Law and of the Covenant that his people were to obey. But when they transgressed he extended his offer of forgiveness. Because the wonder of forgiveness is so hard to grasp Jesus came to spend some time here among his human sisters and brothers (Heb. 2:11,12). In his theological classic, *Embodying Forgiveness,* Gregory Jones explains Jesus was here to embody God's forgiveness. The heavenly forgiver walked among his people and revealed directly what it's all about. He could accept and associate with the scruffiest and the vilest, always with the words of forgiveness on his lips. Here are some examples from Luke's Gospel:

5:20 – To a crippled man on a stretcher before him, "Friend, your sins are forgiven you"

7:48 – To a woman who had tearfully washed his feet, "Your sins are forgiven"

12:10 – To his enemies, "Everyone who speaks a word against the Son of Man will be forgiven"

19:9 – To the little tax collector who wondered aloud if he might have cheated some customers, "Today salvation has come to this house"

In many ways Jesus wove the gospel of forgiveness into his message and ministry. In his teaching on prayer in Matthew's Gospel he taught his disciples how to ask for forgiveness, adding this condition, "If you forgive others their trespasses, your heavenly Father will also forgive you" (6:14). When a paralytic was brought to him for healing Jesus immediately offered forgiveness, before he paid attention to his paralyzed body, "Take heart, your sins are forgiven" (Matt. 9:2). There had not even been a request for forgiveness and there is no evidence to suggest that the patient knew he needed it. But Jesus wanted to grant forgiveness. He saw a healthy conscience as more important than a healthy body. In the passage I mentioned above (Luke 7:36-50) a woman approached Jesus at a banquet table and washed his feet. The host was incredulous – how could a respected teacher like Jesus allow such an extravagant expression of devotion from such a notorious sinner? After roundly scolding his host for his petulance he turned to the woman, "Your sins are forgiven." Before she asked, he blessed her with the gift. At the Last Supper table Jesus explained the symbolic meaning of the cup that he was passing around (Matt. 26:28), "This is my blood of the covenant, which is poured out for many for the forgiveness of sins." I agree with those theologians who suggest that in statements like this his death is a metaphor for his whole incarnational life. His mission, from beginning to end, was to set people free of their sins, as well as from the guilt of their sinning. This ministry of forgiveness came to a dramatic climax when he prayed on the cross, "Father, forgive them; for they do not know what they are doing" (Luke 23:34). With that final expression of God's outreach of absolute forgiving love Jesus left this earthly life.

We should not leave the beautiful gospel of forgiveness without asking, "How can it happen to us?" The answer is that we simply agree to receive it the way we receive any gift. We embrace it in faith and say "Thank-you!" However, accepting forgiveness involves admitting to the shame and embarrassment of our sins. If we can't admit that we are sinners then the offer of forgiveness is an insult. When we say yes to the gift of forgiveness we also have to say yes to our shabby lives. The Bible calls it confession. "If we confess our sins, he is faithful and just and will forgive us our sins" (1 John 1:9 NIV). Confession does not speak of regret or remorse or the begging for mercy. Those responses may be appropriate in our sinfulness. But confession means agreeing, admitting, accepting responsibility, saying yes to the sins we have done. It may feel like drawing the curse of shame upon ourselves. And Volf wonders, "How do we summon the courage to walk into the land of freedom through the gate of shame?" (p. 154). We can do it if we have full confidence in God's infinite love and in the reality of the gift of forgiveness that he has promised.

**For Further Thought and Study**

*1. Read about the destruction of sin in Romans 6:5-10. You will notice that sin has lost its power over us through Christ's death. After this we are still challenged to take personal responsibility for living the new way (v. 11-13). How do you explain the logic?*

*2. Assuming that Luther was correct when he declared that people may be right with God even while there is still sin in their lives, why would we then even bother to be concerned about the sins in which we live?*

*3. What do you say to the concept that God's laws were simply an expression of God's nature? In what way does this change your attitude to those laws?*

*4. Notice the seven metaphors for forgiveness in the following Scriptures: Psalm 103:12; Isaiah 38:18; 43:25; 44:22; Romans 4:7; 4:8; Hebrews 8:12. What is the particular blessing of each?*

*5. Some people who have confessed their sins and have thanked God for forgiveness still feel they are being punished. How would you comfort or encourage them?*

*6. What is easier, to confess to God or to the people we offend? Why is that? How would you answer Volf's question above?*

*7. Let's go back to John the Baptist. He preached a stern message of judgment. Later he was in prison for his strong warnings while Jesus went about extending the grace of forgiveness to all. Imagine yourself going to John in his confusion to explain God's ways to him (Mark 6:17; Matt. 11:2). What would you say?*

# Chapter 8. Hope in Times of Trouble

*If life is a bowl of cherries what am I doing in the pits?* – Erma Bombeck

*Yesterday all my troubles seemed so far away, now it looks as though they're here to stay, oh I believe in yesterday.* – John Lennon and Paul McCartney

*Troubles are often the tools by which God fashions us for better things.* – Henry Ward Beecher

*A mortal, born of woman, few of days and full of trouble, comes up like a flower and withers, flees like a shadow and does not last (*Job 14:1, 2).

*We are afflicted in every way, but not crushed; perplexed, but not driven to despair; persecuted, but not forsaken; struck down, but not destroyed; . . . For while we live, we are always being given up to death for Jesus' sake (*2 Corinthians 4:8-11).

Troubles are with us from birth to death. This is true for all people in all societies. Every day some things don't work right. Someone said, "Trouble is the common denominator of life."

Some optimistic and creative people manage to put a softening spin to it. "I never have any troubles. Just stretches of life that are more interesting than others." I've tried that perspective myself. It helps to see life as a series of challenges that force us to reach deep down for rarely-used resources. In the process we may find we have strengths we did not know about. That's satisfying.

The respected American minister Henry Ward Beecher said, "Troubles are often the tools by which God fashions us for better things." In other words, God can achieve his purposes for our growth through the troubles he allows. I wouldn't be surprised if there is a good bit of truth in that observation.

The entire biblical drama of Job, as exemplified by the quote above, is an attempt to understand why troubles may pile up until we feel we are smothering underneath them. How can such troubles exist in a world in which God is sovereign? All the efforts of Job and his friends to explain Job's troubles seem to go nowhere; at the end they are still stuck with a mystery.

The Psalmists who wrote Israel's worship materials often lament their troubles. At least fifty of the Psalms deal with the troubles of the human life, both the personal and the corporate kind. The depressed mourning of Psalm 38:6 is typical, "I am troubled, I am bowed down greatly; I go mourning all the day long" (KJV). Consequently, the pleas for help, such as Psalm 22:11 are also common, "Do not be far from me, for trouble is near and there is no one to help."

Nobody in the Scriptures has given us such a catalogue of exhausting, near-fatal problems as the early international missionary Paul. In 1 Corinthians 4:9, he laments, "For it seems to me that God has put us apostles on display at the end of the procession, like men condemned to die in the arena (NIV)." And then he expands on that, one painful detail after the other. In the next letter to the same church he speaks of distress, sufferings, and hardships (2 Cor. 1:6-8). Every day he is aware of the threat of death (4:10, 11). The life of a servant of God is marked by hardships and dishonor (6:4-10). And then, since the phony apostles, who are criticizing him, boast of their superior honor, he decides to surpass them by flaunting his particular honor, which means boasting ironically about the incredible series of persecutions and troubles that he recalls (11:21-29).

In view of the sampling of biblical trouble that I have presented above it is surprising, and somewhat distressing, that some Christians can read their Bibles and see only happiness and triumph in their world. And so, they confess an unrealistic faith. Their lives are always just fantastic. They speak as if they are living in a magical bubble above the troubles and tragedies of life. Nothing in the world distresses them and nothing in their personal life troubles them. When I meet such light-hearted Christians I wonder, what have they eaten that blinds them to the experiences of life that are everywhere around them? Stanley Hauerwas sees their kind as being in deep spiritual need, "One of the profoundest forms of faithlessness is the unwillingness to acknowledge our inexplicable suffering and pain" (Kapic, p. 149). And Kelly Kapic counsels wisely, "Let us be unapologetic about our earthiness, about our physicality, since we know that the Creator Lord so made us and declared us good" (Kapic, p. 57).

I hope you agree that it is honest for us believers to speak about troubles. This need not consist of griping about our weaknesses or complaining about the injustices of the Sovereign God. It's just a matter of facing life realistically. There are the natural troubles of life, the troubles that come simply because we are human, the sore muscles when we work, the tension headaches when we've spent too much time at the computer, the occasional winter flu, the threats of cancer or heart problems, and then the inevitable conclusion at the end, death. Most of us have gone through intense sorrow over friends who suffer without relief. The painful afflictions of our own bodies remind us that we are really members of a real world. We do not imagine these realities and no amount of triumphalism will erase them. This is life. We did not invent the idea of trouble. It is real and we are living it. What we are enduring is innate to human existence.

There are the troubles people make for each other. History is replete with horrible examples of what humans do to their fellow people, of what the powerful do to the rich, of how the privileged classes abuse the common folks. Every evening newscast reminds us it is still going on. The news about the unimaginable atrocities that humans perpetrate against each other can drive us into mental distraction if we take them seriously.

Some troubles are simply the result of our own unwise decisions. We create them for ourselves. We can bring contempt and disrespect upon ourselves by *our* scornful attitude to others. We can smash our cars by driving foolishly. We can bring fatal cancer upon ourselves by smoking tobacco. We can wreck our nerves by worrying about troubles that may never come.

And then there are the unique troubles that our life with God may bring with it. "Keeping out of trouble?" the man said to me in the bank atrium. "Not at all," I responded, "My work requires that I get into trouble at least a few times every week." I already mentioned the constant troubles Paul encountered as he travelled to proclaim the good news about Jesus. If he would have stayed in the traditional Jewish enclave of

Jerusalem, loyal to the faith and the lifestyle he had inherited, he could have peacefully twiddled his thumbs until life was done. No problem!

$$* * *$$

The Bible presents us with a dilemma. From beginning to end it encourages us to trust in God and hope for his help. If we pay any attention to the Bible at all, we have to agree that the Bible teaches that God looks after his people. On the other hand, the historical narratives have many painful reminders that God does not always protect even his most devoted servants. John the Baptist preached the truth of God with powerful zeal but then lost his head simply because of one woman's grudge (Mark 6:22-28).

Our daily experiences suggest God's care is mysteriously inconsistent. I may take a trip to the city on icy roads, come home safely, and thank God for protection. Then I recall the smashed car I saw on the roadside and realize at least one other person was not protected. The church prays for its members with cancer; one is healed, one struggles with the disease and disability for years, the other succumbs in a few weeks and is buried. Such examples may even be gleaned out of the experiences of one individual. In November, 2018, while I was writing this chapter the American free-lance missionary Allen Chau was trying to make contact with the primitive residents of Sentinel Island, off the coast of India. Such efforts are illegal under Indian law. After slipping past the police boats guarding the island from intruders he wrote triumphantly in his journal, "God sheltered me and camouflaged me against the coast guard and the navy." Then he paddled to the beach, where the islanders saw him, shot him full of arrows, and buried him in the sand. He thanked God for protection and then he was killed.

The agonizing question remains: How can we hope when the history of God's protection suggests it is sporadic, inconsistent, and unpredictable? To abandon all hope is not an option because living without hope is no longer living. Hopelessness is hell.

I will now present three great hopes that can keep the hell of hopelessness out of our lives. These three hopes are always realistic and viable for every believer at every stage in life. First, there is the hope that God will always be present with us. Some theologians have spoiled this hope. They speak of God's distance, his remoteness, even of his unapproachable aloofness. Their word for it is transcendence.

Focusing only on God's transcendence can lead us in the wrong direction. Think of the God stories that Israel remembered. God came to visit Abraham, he appeared to Isaac and Jacob and promised to make them rich, and he was with Joseph in that Egyptian jail cell. God showed up in a burning bush and assigned Moses to lead his people out of trouble. They would not have thought of God as remote. God was with them as their friend, God was watching and aware, God knew what was going on.

It was in keeping with this great truth that Jesus could promise his friends, just before his final departure, "Now remember, I am with you always, right to the end of the age" (Matt. 28:20). This promise was used later in the letter to the Hebrew believers, reminding them that the Lord had said, "I will never leave you or forsake you." That promise was used to assure them that since they have the Lord with them they have no need to create their own security by selfishly grasping for riches (Heb. 13:5). We need to learn this kind of thinking; the Lord may not keep the bad things out of our lives but he will stay with us in the badness.

The second great hope is that by God's grace we will endure and overcome. Some Christians speak about living triumphantly or victoriously, or they may simply call it "keeping on the sunny side of life." The Bible speaks often of conquering or overcoming. That assumes trouble. Every church letter in Revelation, all seven of them, promise a reward to the churches that will overcome. Then at the end, after the new heaven and new earth have been introduced and God has announced he is making his home among mortals, the concluding promise is, "Those who overcome will inherit these things" (Rev. 21:7).

Overcome? Yes, overcome the temptation to give up, overcome the self-pity that makes life miserable, overcome my complaints about God's unfairness, overcome the lusts that attract me to this present world, overcome my resentments toward my sisters and brothers who are wealthier than I am, and overcome my unforgiving attitude toward those who have hurt me.

Overcome? Yes, it means growing in grace and gentleness and friendliness and patience even though the problems continue to plague us with relentless stubbornness.

Overcome? Yes, it means continuing with a smile even though nobody can assure us that the physical handicaps or mental weaknesses will ever vanish while we are in this life.

Overcome? Yes, but it may mean heeding the comfort that the Lord had for Paul when he griped about his thorn in the flesh, "My grace is sufficient for you" (2 Cor. 12:9). There will be grace enough and we shall overcome!

The third great hope is that at the end all things will be well. In the long run all trouble will turn out, right side up, for God's people. For the believer any suffering, hardship, or anxiety is never the last word. Not even death. Sometimes the transformation of the trouble comes already in this life. This is illustrated by the life of Joseph, who was hated by his brothers, sold into slavery, imprisoned on a trumped-up charge, forgotten in jail for years, but emerged as an honored gentleman to take over the leadership of the entire nation. This type of thing may actually happen. However, the Scriptures hold before us the assurance that, regardless of how it looks here, in the spiritual dimension of eternity all will be well for all of God's people. You can read about it in Revelation 21.

In the mean time the believer has the right to look ahead in faith and relax in the attitude to life expressed by the apostle Paul, "For this momentary light affliction is preparing for us an eternal weight of glory beyond all measure" (2 Cor. 4:17). "I consider that the sufferings of this present time are not worth comparing with the glory about to be revealed to us" (Rom. 8:18). "We know that all things work together for good for those who love God" (Rom. 8:28). Holding to such a hope one can always feel at peace. When some issues of this age have not ended well Christians can always tell themselves that matters have not really ended yet. The story isn't over; the final sentence has not yet been written; the final period is not yet in place; there is more to come.

All this means that we need the long view, the vision of the eternal, invisible, spiritual new dimension of the future. However, since God is with us now and loves us as physical humans, we should hope as the Psalmist did, "I believe that I shall see the goodness of the Lord in the land of the living." However, that ancient poet realizes that living with such a confidence takes a durable patience, "Wait for the Lord; be strong, and let your heart take courage; wait for the Lord" (Ps. 27:13, 14).

We are not saying that trouble is good or that we should desire troubles. We are not claiming that we have to suffer in order to become aware of God or that suffering people are necessarily more spiritual than others. But I have noticed that suffering people are sometimes more thankful than they were before they suffered. In other words, while trouble is never God's will for us it may be the doorway to a deeper life of faith and joy with him. When Paul heard the word of the Lord, "My grace is sufficient for you," he responded gratefully, "In that case, I will be content with weaknesses, insults, hardships, persecutions, and calamities for Christ's sake." That's the spirit God admires!

$$* * *$$

Hope is not achieved through the power of positive thinking or by any other mental gymnastics. It's a gift from God as we trust in the promises of the Word. Normally, hope will be the result of living together in the community of the Spirit. The Spirit inspires us to speak to God for the suffering folks around us and then to turn to the suffering ones and speak to them for God. The Hebrew Psalmists did this by reminding their people to recall God's faithfulness in the past. In fact, as we read the Psalms we gain the impression that the purpose of the historical narratives of the Scriptures is not so much to provide a record of human successes and failings as to retain the memory of the Lord's gracious goodness. The healing and helping stories in the Old Testament provide us with glimpses of God's caring concern and of his freedom to provide practical help. These stories of the past prepare us for the ministry of healing, helping, and comforting that marked the life of Jesus. Not only did Jesus' miracles identify him as the same Lord who had lived with the earlier community of believers, they confirmed that the God of Israel is actually the Father of all peoples.

The Lord may allow pain and suffering, he may seem to be silent and withdrawn, but he never forsakes or abandons his people. The stories that chronicle human sin and its resultant miseries are interspersed with bright spots of hope and confidence in God's caring presence. These recollections of God's past goodness encourage God's people to anticipate future grace and goodness as well. The Psalms admit the perplexity of suffering. They do not attempt to explain why God may act here and why he may seem to be withdrawn there. The wounded and despairing believers are never belittled or despised for their anguish. The troubles are real, but they don't change the trustworthiness of the Lord.

The writing prophets of Israel had many sharp and dire warnings of judgment. Recently I browsed through all the sixteen prophetic books of the Old Testament and found that every writer at some point inserts a beautiful sprig of hope in the message. The strongest promises come in Isaiah, Jeremiah, and Ezekiel. All of them wrote to the same dilemma. Jerusalem, the city where God once had his home (so they thought), had been sacked and demolished. God had seemed to be impotent to protect his place. The leadership class had been marched away as captives to Babylon and those who remained functioned as a distant subservient province of the powerful northern empire. For the leaders who had been deported and for the defeated survivors at home the prophets proclaimed in agreement, "There is hope!"

The challenge we face in the difficulties of these times is how do we honestly affirm the troubles, but faithfully hold on to our hope that God will be faithful. For the original disciples of Jesus this paradox was resolved by the resurrection of Jesus. In spite of his full trust in the Father and his total obedience to his heavenly mission, he was misunderstood, criticized, judged to be a blasphemer, and then executed like a common criminal. This happened in this world right in God's presence. After the nefarious deeds of that dismal day were done the disciples were completely devastated and confused. Nothing that they had seen and learned over the past three years helped them to make sense of the moral darkness in which they now found themselves. At that point God's world just made no sense. But then came the resurrection! It seems to me they never tried very hard to sort out the philosophical mysteries of the death of Jesus. They were content to declare that, in some way, Jesus died for us. He died because we are sinful people. But he is alive now as we will also one day be alive. And so, I suggest that even if we cannot make sense of the present darkness and see no possible solution to the prevalence of international injustice and the consequent miseries of innocent people, we can still in full integrity keep on counting on God to look after his world.

To summarize this chapter, I remind you that whatever we make of our troubled circumstances, the New Testament council is that we need not worry. Listen to Paul's elegant advice, "Do not worry about anything, but in everything by prayer and supplication with thanksgiving let your requests be known to God. And the peace of God, which surpasses all understanding, will guard your hearts and your minds in Christ Jesus" (Phil. 4:6, 7). We can live in peace because we can always approach God in prayer.

I have already mentioned that some people take great comfort in their conviction that "God is in control." That seems to solve the worst problem. That simple concept serves as their Christian mantra. The Bible study group may have struggled with some horrible, unsolvable injustice going on somewhere, to which someone adds piously, "Well, at least we know that God is in control." With that they all go home to sleep well. I see no evidence in the Scriptures or in history that God controls ungodly people or evil powers. God did not create the world to control it. People were given the freedom to be good or bad. And the extent to which that freedom can be used to create havoc and misery is downright scary.

However, the source of our hope lies in God's assurance that he has not abandoned his creation. He is present everywhere with his incredible patience and grace. Recently I noticed that the book of Deuteronomy, with its emphasis on the laws of God that Israel is to obey, uses the formula, "that it may go well with you." It's there ten times. This sums up God's attitude; in his deep compassion he wants it to be well with his people.

Finally, I add that it is not necessary for us to understand in what way God may help us and guide us through our troubles. And even though Peter says we should always be ready to speak up when we are asked about our hope (1 Peter 3:15), we don't need to explain the details of God's expected help. We are simply invited to hope. Whatever God may do or not do in response to our prayers for help, we always honor God when we turn to him in hope.

### For Further Thought and Study

*1. What kinds of troubles in your personal, family, or community affairs tend to worry you? What kind of troubles have been resolved by your own efforts, and where did prayer seem to be effective?*

*2. What kinds of national or international evil bother you? In what sense is it right that we be concerned over such impersonal issues?*

*3. What kind of spiritual blessings have you gained through the troubles that you encountered?*

*4. How do you respond to the author's underlying assumption that God has created people with the freedom to do wrong and bring grief upon themselves?*

*5. Read a few selected Psalms that deal with God's help in times of trouble, Psalm 9:9, 31:7, 34:7, 50:15; 77:14. What do you learn from these testimonies if divine help? Read about God's providential care of nature in Psalm104:27-30, and note that the goodness is interspersed by the reality of death. How do you cope with that reality?*

*6. Read about the Apostle Paul's troubles in this sequence, 2 Corinthians, 4:7-11, 4:16-18, 11:23-33, 12:7b-10. What principles for dealing with trouble do you discern?*

# Chapter 9. Hope in the Presence of Death

*Christians are Easter people living from and toward that Easter experience of a new creation.* – Hans Schwarz

*While I thought that I was learning how to live, I have been learning how to die.* -- Leonardo da Vinci

*Death, be not proud, though some have called thee mighty and dreadful, for thou art not so.* – John Donne

*Yet we do not even know what tomorrow will bring. What is your life? For you are a mist that appears for a little while and then vanishes* (James 4:14).

*But in fact Christ has been raised from the dead, the first fruits of those who have died. . . . For as all die in Adam, so all will be made alive in Christ* (1 Cor. 15:20, 22).

From the common troubles that we encounter throughout life I move on to the biggest trouble of all, the mother of all troubles – death. I have occasionally been at a bedside when some good friend died. I have, over the course of my pastoral life, conducted over two hundred funerals. Each of these meant sitting with bereaved people, listening to their stories of death, and planning some suitable service that would properly honor the deceased.

Death is no fun; dead bodies are not amusing or interesting. I received an urgent call from a church family to come to the emergency room at the local hospital; their son had been picked up somewhere, dead. When I walked into the silent, somber room the coroner was just completing his cursory examination of the corpse. Knowing him by name, I asked, "So what would you say happened?" He replied curtly, "I would say his heart stopped." I got the message; he had no interest and no need to talk about the case to me.

I've often talked to dying people in hospital rooms; that's what pastors are taught to do. A man in the late stages of leukemia thanked me warmly for talking about dying, his wife wouldn't. A woman in the hallway asked me to talk to her husband about dying because she couldn't; when I gently invited him to talk about dying, he immediately clammed up and would not say a further word to me. Another man almost shouted at me when I mentioned death, "That's evil, that's the devil's thing, don't speak about it." I took a deep breath and asked if we could speak about heaven. "Fine," he said. Do you sense the irony? You can't get to heaven without dying. And then there was the man, who had always been proud of being strong and tough, who told me with a gleeful smile from his hospital bed, "I'm dying; my doctor told me my heart would last no more than another two weeks."

I've wondered, which is the right attitude? Mostly, however, I've been impressed by the calm and serene spirit with which many dying people are able to discuss their departure. On several occasions a patient has told me they are ready, whenever it comes. And then they have turned to me, "There, now let's talk about the funeral service." I've wondered, is this a special gift that God gives to soften the last days and to lighten the grief of the survivors? And I've wondered what kind of attitude I would take if I would have to consciously reflect on the approach of an imminent death.

I love life; I enjoy living, I thank God almost every day for the privilege of being alive. In many ways I find this to be a wonderful world – the forests, the fields, the mountains, the seas, the creatures, and the seven billion people, the hundreds of different cultures, each different from the other. I often marvel at the incredible idea God had when he created life. I enjoy living so much that I would like to live forever, and there's the problem. In order to live forever, in order to move over into the life of the eternal dimension, I'll have to die here. The Bible has two exceptions to that: There once was a man called Enoch of whom we read, "He was no more because God took him" (Gen. 5:24). And then there was the fearless, fighting prophet Elijah whom God also took straight to heaven; they only found his coat, that's all he left (2 Kings 2). But normally whenever someone goes to heaven, the body stays behind, dead. You've noticed that. So far there is no *other* way to there from here.

There's a lot of death in the Bible, the death of old age, of sickness, of torture, of murder, of warfare, of suicide, of genocide. Along with that there is the shock, the pain, the grieving, the terror and the anger, the questioning of God and the confusion about the inconsistent nature of divine providence. It's all there. That's why some can't stand reading the Bible; it's too much like the daily newspaper. The Bible is realistic about the nature of human life because we need to learn to live with life as it comes. Death is never far away in this wonderful, beautiful world that is teeming with the incredible mystery of life. It started with the first family. One son resented the fact that his brother seemed to be more popular with God than he was and so he clubbed him to death. The simple way to solve a problem! With that he showed his contempt for both, for God and his brother.

Alongside of all the bad and sad news the Bible also provides us with all kinds of hopeful stuff. Starting early, near the beginning of human history, we read that Abraham died in a good old age and was gathered to his people. That sounds quite benign, doesn't it? When he left here he joined his people who had departed earlier. And that point is important; from earliest times it was understood that when people die they *go* somewhere. The stuff about heaven and hell, about blessedness or lostness, and the complexities of resurrection and judgment come later.

Jesus once told his disciples, in preparation for the persecution that their loyalty to him would inevitably entail, "Do not fear those who kill the body but cannot kill the soul" (Matt. 10:28). That not only impresses us with its nonchalance, but fascinates us with its assumption about the human person. The enemies may kill the body but they cannot kill the soul. There's a difference; one is mortal, the other isn't. We will return to this insight later.

The apostle Paul seemed to live fearlessly. He was in danger all the time. Every day he was sacrificing his life for the sake of Jesus (2 Cor. 4:11). But he never wallows in worries or sinks into self-pity. When he was discussing his future prospects as a prisoner of the Imperial authorities in Rome he wrote rather casually, "For to me, living is Christ and dying is gain" (Phil. 1:21).

However, in another context the same apostle writes of death as the last enemy that will have to be destroyed (1 Cor. 15:26). Then he goes on to taunt death as if death is an enemy who will soon lose all its lethal powers, "Where, O death, is your victory? Where, O death, is your sting?" (v. 55). To abandon once and for all the soft and sentimental notion that death is sweet and good we listen to the writer of Hebrews who explains that Jesus visited the earthly abode of humankind to "destroy the one who has the power of death, that is, the devil, and free those who all their lives were held in slavery by the fear of death" (Heb. 2:14, 15). Because Jesus has been here and because he offers to fill our lives with his presence, death need not terrorize us anymore. We are free to live in hope.

In spite of the reality of death the Bible offers us an abundance of hope, piled up along with the bad, dark news. You find it in Job and in some of the Psalms and in the visions the prophets had, especially Isaiah. You find it in the teachings of Jesus and in the testimonies of Paul and Peter and John, especially in the last big concluding vision that we call Revelation. There it stands, "Death will be no more" (Rev. 21:4). Simple and clear as that! And when death is finally banished, gone will also be the tears, the mourning, and the pain. It's all one miserable package and God will fix the whole works. That's the big promise and that gives us grounds for hoping. And now we will explore the details.

* * *

I admit that all this good news is not well organized, it's sort of helter-skelter, jumbled up. It can become quite confusing if you want to arrange it all in a simple systematic way. Some people feel truth should be clear and specific with all the details fitting together in a nice comprehensive order. If you need such a coherent exactitude you will have problems with the last chapters of this book. And you will have even bigger problems with the Bible, at least if you read it with care. Professor Peter Enns has written a book about the sin of certainty. I would not put it that severely, but I do agree that craving for certainty can knock all the hope and joy out of a person's life. Such a person is also, usually, a pain to live with.

The Bible is a living book. Its words were written for many different kinds of people over a very long period of time. That's why I say the Bible is alive; it keeps on growing with time. We are alive and we also grow with time; all living things grow. And when there is growth there is change. Trees change as they grow, your body changes as it grows, and your thinking will change as you grow. But people who are totally certain cannot change; their growing mechanism is stuck in a rut. They end up being poor, shriveled up, dried up, frozen up specimens of humanity, and usually unhappy to boot. So, if the passion for certainty can be dangerous, troublesome, and leave you stranded in a dry creek bed, then what? Then we have hope!

Hope is an essential aspect of Christian faith; it is faith, looking ahead into the future. "Faith has to do with things that are not seen and hope with things that are not at hand." That's how Thomas Aquinas put it. Hope means looking ahead, out beyond this time and this space, and believing in what's out there. It means trusting in a good future so strongly that it changes our outlook on everything in the present. In hope we don't deny the dismal, oppressive features of this life, but we are able to look beyond all the darkness here to the glorious brightness out there.

Some believers seem to find strong solace in the presence of death because they tell themselves God is the Great Manager of all things and nothing will happen without his approval. That comforting thought takes the anxiety out of their life. They can go to bed and sleep in peace because God is in charge. I'm glad for them. However, their view of life does not work for me because every day I hear of dreadful, awful things that happen in this world that God is supposedly managing. As I've already mentioned in a previous chapter, absolutely horrible things may happen even to those who strongly believe in God. I have on several occasions sat with shocked, grieving people whose spouses went to bed in good health and never woke up. That's life! And death! The idea that the people of God are always safe is a cruel myth. My comfort is that whatever happens God will be there with me; I will never be on my own.

Whatever view one takes of God, one can't help wondering sometimes, is this how the Sovereign Lord manages the world? Maybe we are working with the wrong concepts. Let's rather say the Lord is here in this world in the midst of all the anger, the violence, the pain, and the death. God participates with us in this whole unholy mess. And God can look ahead much farther than we can; he sees the end. And from his position of infinite prescience he announces that it will all end well.

Let's look for a minute at how we live our lives. We start out with optimism in the years of our youth, then we try to live realistically in the adult years, and finally, nearing the end we slide into weariness and gloom. We have good times and bad times, but then we fade out, or flame out. And it's over. We will be gone. Humanly speaking it looks rather pointless. As I wrote these words I wondered if they were too dark and gloomy. Then I noticed that Matthew McCullough has just written a book, *Remember Death*. He writes, "Before you long for a life that is imperishable you must accept that you are perishing with everything you care about. You must recognize that everything you might accomplish or acquire in this world is already fading away." The subtitle of the book is "The Surprising Path to Living Hope." That's where we are heading with this chapter, and so we carry on.

Hope is a gift, a gift that comes to us from God. In a very important sense, hope is *the* Christian thing. We have the right to live in hope and speak about hope. Our Christian hope is not something we generate ourselves; it's not a homemade product. I realize some unbelievers are incredibly optimistic; everything is always fantastic for them. I don't know how they do it. I also know unbelievers can be very funny, even about human miseries such as death.

If it were up to my mind to figure out some hope for Iraq, Syria, Afghanistan, South Sudan, Gaza, and Yemen, for all the impoverished mothers in the world who watch their starving children die on their laps, for all the women who were raped as little girls, treated as slaves, and abused by every man they've ever met, for all my aging, weakening relatives, I would be as miserable as actor Robin Williams was (He has been called the funniest person of all time, but ended his own life in 2014). But it's not up to me to make hope, I just open my heart in faith and receive the gift. It's sent along to us through the prophets of old times and the apostles of Jesus. In fact, no one was as explicit about promising hope as Jesus himself. I don't think I've ever heard anybody say it, but we could say Jesus stepped out of heaven to bring some hope to earth. He never used the term, but he was brimful of it. He once showed up in a home where they had just finished a funeral and announced, "I am the resurrection and the life. Those who believe in me, even though they die, will live, and everyone who lives and believes in me will never die" (John

11:25, 26). Let that assurance, from the one who knows it all, lodge deeply at the heart of your hoping.

\* \* \*

Now, what happens when a person dies? What hope is there for the dying person and for those who wait and grieve? I will here present three answers that Christian scholars have given. First of all, there is the basic concept, taught by modern psychology, that the person is one indivisible unit. When a person dies that person is totally dead. There are no immortal remains. The late Stanley Grenz, one of my favorite theologians, seems to hold to this position. Discussing the state of the dead he says they are "held by God" and that God "retains the personhood of the dead" until the end-time resurrection (p. 596). He mentions this hope occasionally but always seems cautiously vague about it. The clearest statement on this position that I have found is by the German theologian Wolfhart Pannenberg. He says the New Testament teaching on resurrection is based on

> the assumption that our life, whose history ends in the moment of death, passes away in that moment from our experience, but not from the eternal presence of God. In God's memory our individual life is preserved. Thus there is no element of our earthly existence that would escape death in order to guarantee our continued existence beyond death, but only God is able, because of his unlimited power, to preserve our temporal lives in his memory and grant them a new form of existence of their own" (Braaten and Jenson, p. 8).

The problem with this view, from a biblical perspective, is that both Testaments speak as if some form of conscious life continues after death.

The second view is based on the common Christian concept that a person consists of two components, the spiritual and the physical. Jesus' words in Matthew 10:28, quoted above, may be understood in this way. This view is that when the body dies the spiritual component (some call it the soul), in which the full human personality resides, continues in conscious existence, not in heaven but in some intermediate state, waiting for the resurrection. My earliest teachers promoted this view. As I understand him, the British New Testament scholar N. T. Wright argues for this view in *Surprised by Hope*. He sums it up as "there is life after life after death." He means there is resurrected life to come for those who are already alive in the intermediate stage. Critics of this view say the idea that a human consists of two distinct elements is a pagan Greek idea and if the Bible speaks thus it is influenced by its pagan environment. However, John W. Cooper argues strongly for such dualism. He speaks freely about the person "coming apart at death." He reasons that the fact that early Greek philosophy happens to teach the same does not falsify what the writers of our inspired Scriptures posit. As I see it, a weakness of this view is that it's hard to find a thing like an intermediate state in the Bible. It seems to have been invented to accommodate our need for some kind of interim parking place for the soul until the time of the resurrection comes by. Further, it's unclear in what way this imaginary intermediate state differs from the heaven that will be entered at the end of earthly time. I suggest that our biblical hope does not require it.

The third view suggests that people are transformed at the point of death into their eternal form. Dying means entry into heaven. Among the theologians whom I have followed, Brian Hebblethwaite of Cambridge is perhaps the most clear and explicit about this. In response to the positions presented above he says, "It seems much more plausible to think that God raises persons when they die to the life of the world to come. . . . Resurrection itself is best hoped for immediately as we commend our own lives or those of others into God's hands at death" (p. 212, 3). Those who hold to this view remind us that in John's Gospel those who are loyal to Jesus Christ are seen as already having eternal life here and now. They already possess now the life of the age to come. Death is then merely the full transmission into the life in which they already belong. This eliminates the need to invent an intermediate stage. I know this view has philosophical and psychological problems too, but it is simple and uncomplicated compared to the other views. And in fact, anything that we envision about the future dimension looks mysterious to earthly human eyes.

Gerhard Lohfink refers frequently to death as an encounter with God. In death the believer comes face to face with the One who is the resurrection and the life. His formula for the believer's future is "resurrection in death." This concept of encountering God in death will come up again in the next chapter.

The New Testament has four brief but fascinating vignettes of truth that seem to support this third position. I've already mentioned Jesus and his friends in Bethany. The two sisters were in deep sorrow because their brother had died four days ago. Jesus spoke to their grief, "I am the resurrection and the life. Those who believe in me, even though they die, will live, and everyone who lives and believes in me will never die" (John 11:25, 26). This sounds as if dying people keep on living, as if they move directly through death into their future life.

We encounter the second picture when we read about Jesus on the cross. The criminal on the cross beside him asked to be remembered in Jesus' kingdom. Obviously, he understood something about Jesus that many had not grasped. Jesus simply promised, "Today you will be with me in Paradise" (Luke 23:43). "Paradise" is so rarely used in the Bible that it is difficult to determine precisely what it meant. In any case Jesus expects that he and his dying neighbor will both arrive in their next home later that day.

And then there was Paul, languishing in prison somewhere, and contemplating the possibilities of gaining freedom, or of being executed. "I am hard pressed between the two: my desire is to depart and to be with Christ, for that would be far better," he reasoned (Phil. 1:23). Again, the words sound as if he anticipated a direct passage from prison into the presence of Christ.

Another indicator that has moved me toward the third view is what I read out of 2 Corinthians 5:1-10. The apostle speaks here as if earthly life is like a tent that will be destroyed. But he is looking forward to a new house from God, eternal in the heavens. Then he switches the metaphor and speaks as if it's time to discard his old clothing. It is not that he wants to be unclothed, but rather to be dressed up in better clothes. The crucial line that describes what will happen is that "what is mortal may be swallowed up by life." He seems to expect to move from his current mortality into the new and better life. My cautious conclusion is that, although the third view has its problems, a non-critical reading of the New Testament makes it seem the likeliest.

I mentioned that Stanley Grenz holds to the first view, and he does not like this third view because in the Scriptures resurrection is always future and it's always celebrated as a coming community event. To this we can say that there is the subjective and then the objective aspect of resurrection hope. The individual believer is resurrected at death, and then when Jesus returns there will be one grand, culminating resurrection party. Those who have already been personally blessed with the new life of eternity will return with Christ to meet those who will be transformed at the second coming of Jesus Christ (1 Cor. 15:51, 52; 1 Thess. 4:14). In other words, there is the immediate, personal experience of resurrection at the point of death, which will be followed by the entire community of Christ celebrating the eternal life of the new age at his return. Individually the resurrection is immediate, collectively the resurrection comes at the end.

I sense that our reluctance to embrace the third position may be due to the fact that, in whatever case, resurrection is an inexplicable mystery. It's easier to believe in mysteries if they can be pushed out into the dim future than if they happen unseen around us. I've assured my students that all three views can be defended with biblical arguments. All hold to the basic essentials; there will be a resurrection of the full human being, and the future is totally in the hands of God.

* * *

Let's now use the biblical teaching about the resurrection to celebrate our blessedness. I start with the beautiful benediction of Psalm 144:15, "Blessed are the people whose God is the Lord" (NIV). I have wondered what would be the proper contemporary term to use instead of the venerable biblical word "blessed." I've decided the happy exclamation I sometimes hear, "Good for you!" would have the same connotation. And so, I exclaim now, "Good for the people who know God in their bereavement."

Good? Yes, because people who know God have the privilege of prayer. They may not feel like having company and listening to kind words, but they can pray. They may be totally confused but they can pray because God doesn't mind confusion. They may be angry at God, but they can pray their anger. That's okay with God. Obviously, we cannot protect ourselves from pain and sorrow by praying. Sicknesses and old age and the final closure eventually come to everybody. Death and sorrow are very human things and human things happen to all people. But those who know God can turn to God in prayer and pour it out there. Good for them!

Good? Yes, because they can expect God's friendly presence throughout the grief process. The inner working of the Holy Spirit seems like a mystery to me. There have been tight-fisted, covetous people who turned beautifully generous. I've known people who were angry at everybody, but then turned into gracious friends. I've known tense and worried people who somehow learned to live in peace. I've known bitter people who refused to forgive but then were moved by the Spirit to let go and forgive anyway. How does the Spirit of God perform these wonders with us struggling people? And then there are those who feel so battered by the pain of grief that they think they will never be happy again. But the miracle-working Spirit is with them and as they walk through their grief the pain is somehow changed into a new strength and a higher purpose in life. Some of you know about this better than I do, for you've been there. Good for you!

Good? Yes, because they can have hope in the resurrection if they are capable of such a faith. Hope means to look ahead by faith. Hope means expecting the good so strongly that one enjoys it before it happens. Hope means counting on God so firmly that one feels one is right in God's presence. Someone has said, "Everybody wants to go to heaven, but nobody wants to die." I'm suggesting that with true hope one can even agree to die. People who have hope can see things to which others may be oblivious. Hope is the Christian thing; Christians have the right to hope because they have God.

Look at the biblical data that can feed our hope. First, there is the general, most inclusive promise, "If the Spirit of him who raised Jesus from the dead is living in you, he who raised Christ from the dead will also give life to your mortal bodies" (Rom. 8:11). You notice that this agrees well with the third position above and with Jesus' words in John 11:26, "Everyone who lives and believes in me will never die." In a sense, those who live in Jesus, believe in him, and have the Spirit with them will not die at all. They already have the life of eternity.

In 1 Corinthians 15 the apostle discusses our future in terms of the resurrection motif. First, he reminds us that our hope is based on the resurrection of Jesus. If Jesus had not been raised we would have no faith (v. 17). Then he explains that Christ in his resurrection is the prototype of all those who will be raised after him (most versions use the word "firstfruits" here). What God did with the dead Jesus is what God plans to do with all of Jesus' people. We have all inherited mortal bodies that are destined to die, but we already have new life in Christ

(v. 22). Paul expects we will wonder what the new body of the future will be like. He doesn't try to answer that one, but explains there are many different types of bodies, each having its own glory. He seems to say, "Don't worry, God is creative enough to provide us with something very good and eternally appropriate (v. 35-41). Then he abandons all caution and declares, "There is a physical body, there is also a spiritual body" (v. 44). He never entertains the idea that we might exist as disembodied spirits. In this life we have physical bodies; for the life of the eternal future we will have spiritual bodies. If we need any more information than this we can look at the resurrected Jesus. Not only does Jesus live the new life, he models what *we* will be like in the new life. Now we are of the dust as Adam was, then we will be like Jesus, the man of heaven (v. 49). Good for us! "Blessed are the people whose God is the Lord."

### *For Further Thought and Study*

*1. Does death seem like a friend or a foe? What is your gut response? Upon further reflection, in what situation would each term seem to fit?*

*2. After reading the opening paragraphs, how do you think you will respond when death seems near?*

*3. What have you seen, heard, or thought of that influences the way you feel about the three views of death that the author discusses?*

*4. How important is the promise of resurrection life to you? Explain your interest or lack of interest in it?*

*5. Read what Jesus had to say about the resurrection in John 5:28, 29, 6:39-54, 11:25, 26. What do you learn?*

*6. Read about the test question the Sadducees had of Jesus (Matt. 22:23-28). What do you learn from Jesus' answer (v.29-32)?*

*7. Read 1 Corinthians 15:35-49. What does the passage say to you? With what questions does it leave you? Which is the most comforting detail?*

# Chapter 10. Hope for Grace Beyond the Grave

*"Hope is a passion for the possible."* – Soren Kierkegaard

*"Surely a God of infinite power and wisdom could give optimal grace to all people and give them the best chance to accept the truth of the gospel and be saved. Death is hardly a barrier that such a God could not overcome."* – Jerry Walls.

*"The gates of the holy city are depicted as being open day and night (Isa. 60:11; Rev. 21:25), which means that access to the throne of grace is a continuing possibility. . . . Even when one is in hell one can be forgiven."* -- Donald Bloesch

*"Consequently he is able for all time to save those who approach God through him, since he always lives to make intercession for them"* (Heb. 7:25).

*"Let anyone who wishes take the water of life as a gift"* (Rev. 22:17).

I was sitting at my computer, trying to think of some nice words to say at the funeral of a good friend. The title of a book lying nearby caught my eye, *Long Night's Journey into Day*. That became the theme for my devotional then. Now I suggest that title describes my personal journey, from the horrible, hopeless, gruesome things I was taught to believe about those who have died without faith, to a position of tentative hope. It feels like a trip from night into day. With this chapter I am not telling you what you must believe. This chapter is a testimony, my personal story, sharing how my hope has grown over the years. I realize some readers will find my hope unacceptable and I am not writing to convert them to my viewpoint, but to explain another important aspect of *my* hoping. This is *my* testimony of *my* long night's journey into day.

One of the first funerals I conducted was for a twenty-year-old man, the son of church members, who was involved in a drunken race down the highway that ended in the total smash-up of their little sports car, and with both occupants instantly dead. I preached on hope. But I could only speak about hope that the life of the bereaved would go on in spite of the horrific family disaster. I wished I could say some comforting words about the deceased, but the teaching I had received left me with no kind words that I could say to the family about their son.

Many years later, a lot older and maybe a little wiser, I was having a little devotional service with a ninety-year-old in his nursing home room. It was the Easter season and I was talking about the joy of the resurrection. He interrupted me bitterly. "There is no joy in the resurrection. I have three sons who are not walking with Jesus. If there will be a resurrection they will be raised, only to be damned to hell. I can't stand the thought." I struggled with the gospel I was proclaiming; how could I word it so that he would receive some comfort for his hellish anxiety?

Around the same time, I called on a recently bereaved ninety-two-year-old widower. He confronted me immediately with the truth, "Now that my good wife has died, I can tell you that I am an atheist." He gave me three precise reasons for his unbelief. One was that he could not believe in a God who would, for thousands of years, allow people to be born, to die, and to be damned to hell simply because they happened to live before there was a Savior. For such cruel management of the world he had no use; it could not be true. It would be nice to say I helped him. I don't know if I did, even though I called on him many times during the last few years of his life. The doctrines he had been taught, by his mother and by the preachers in the church he had attended as a youth, seemed to be permanently etched into his worldview.

What's the problem? Our first teachers, and most of the faith statements of the churches in which we grew up, taught us that those who die without faith in Jesus Christ are banished to a hell of fire in which they will suffer forever, with no respite or remittance ever. The respected London Pastor Charles Spurgeon once preached,

> When thou diest thy soul shall be tormented alone; that will be a hell
> for it. But at the day of judgment thy body will join thy soul, and then

thou wilt have twin hells, thy soul sweating drops of blood, and thy body suffering with agony. In fire exactly like that which we have on earth thy body will live, asbestos like, forever unconsumed, all thy veins roads for the feet of Pain to travel on, every nerve a string on which the Devil shall forever play his diabolical tune of hell's unutterable lament!" (Leckie, p.104).

I am not surprised that such surrealistic imaginations have been a blot on Christian theology and have caused many sensitive people to turn from the Christian faith. I suggest that the traditional view of hell has probably created more atheists than anything else that Christians have said or done.

Some of our respected theological forefathers, such as Thomas Aquinas and Jonathan Edwards, even saw hellfire as a source of blessing for those in heaven (Whale, p. 164). Heavenly entertainment! Such incredible convictions are our theological heritage!

Death-bed conversions have been accepted and even celebrated, but the moment a person stops breathing the evangelical verdict is that it's all over with grace and mercy and compassion and the love of God. "As the tree falls so shall it lie." Death is the end; it ends all opportunities for repentance, forgiveness, and growth.

My impression is that few Christians actually think deeply about hell; the human mind can't even imagine the horror of it. James Packer, of whom I think as the staunchest fundamentalist professor I've met, agrees. In an essay in *Crux* he wrote that hell will be far worse than it sounds like; it will be so horrible that we better not even try to imagine it. We should just affirm it, and then go on with life.

In other words, we are taught that God has created a cosmic concentration camp for unbelievers that seems to be far worse than anything the Nazis or Communists ever designed. At a higher level of education my Calvinistic professors with doctoral titles explained that unbelief alone is such a heinous sin against Almighty God that an eternal inferno is actually a mercy. They also insisted that God *has* to punish sin, regardless of how ignorant, unfortunate, deceived, or abused the sinner may happen to be. That's God's moral duty, they declared. What does one do with such a theological foundation? Some go crazy. Some commit suicide. Some turn to atheism. Some turn their back on the horror and focus only on the sunny side of life. I chose to reach for hope. I found enough to allow me to keep on teaching, preaching, and smiling.

I feel I should explain the paragraphs above. This not a chapter about hell; it's about hope. However, the traditional concept of hell can be such a hope-destroying factor in one's life that some attention to it seems necessary. I don't recall that I've ever been afraid of going to hell. However, the dark reality that most of the people of previous eras, and most of the people around me today, are headed to an eternal inferno without any chance of a break hung like a black, bleak cloud over my life and ministry. And then, one day the sun broke through.

We were spending a Sabbatical leave at Oxford University in the fall of 1991. Every day I was in the Bodleian Library, pursuing my favorite hobby, reading theology. There I discovered a tradition of which I had been unaware. There has been an ongoing viewpoint on the sidelines of the church from the first centuries till the present, that the infernal fires mentioned in the Bible are figurative references to the purifying effects of the love of God in eternity. This would mean that people could, after death, be cleansed and forgiven. I cautiously decided to take my stand with this minority, and I thanked God for the new possibility of hope. I said "cautiously" because I was afraid of making God more gracious than he is. George Macdonald knew of the same fear; he wrote about people who have a strong belief in God, but "seem greatly to fear imagining Him better than he is" (p. 93). Further, I felt uneasy because I realize that the horror of hell has been used in my evangelical tradition as a motivator for missions. I overcame that fear when I noticed that Jesus did not use hell to inspire his disciples. He taught them to preach the message of the kingdom of God as *good* news. I also noticed that the apostle Paul has no mention of hell, or even of eternal lostness, in his major teaching document, his letter to the Romans.

And then I was cautious because some of my fellow church people think that a gruesome eternal hell serves as a deterrent against careless, lustful, sinful living. I realize that John Wesley turned eighteenth century England upside down with his incessant call to "flee from the wrath to come." It worked. It also worked for John the Baptizer (Matt. 3:7). But my impression is that hellfire preaching has lost its punch; it is basically seen as a sick joke in Western society today.

Some Christians have no problem with the traditional view of eternal punishment. Others realize that the pictures of eternal damnation in the NT, if taken seriously and literally, are difficult to integrate into the gospel of grace. Especially if one feels compelled to believe it of a child or a friendly neighbor or a friend who rejected the Christian faith because of abuse at the hands of a Christian parent or church leader. Such people may feel compelled to keep on believing in the unimaginable because of their loyalty to the inerrancy of the Scriptures, but think about it as little as possible.

I pause for a few more words of personal explanation. I remind you, as I already said above, that this chapter is not doctrinal teaching; it is a testimony. I am not trying to convert anybody to my view; conversion is the Spirit's thing. It's a report of my experience. This is my story; this is what kept me from following Bart Ehrman or Christopher Hitchens into the wilderness of theological skepticism. This is what *The Globe and Mail* calls an "Opinion Piece." Please consider that as you read. I expect that some people will read this chapter and decide I have become a pathetic nut case. But I have already discovered that many of my sisters and brothers in the Christian faith have longed intensely for the kind of hope I discuss here.

We came home from our Sabbatical time at Oxford University and a few months later a leader in our church told me, "Arden, you are a happier person than you used to be." I did not think it was safe to tell him the source of my new joy. In fact, I've told my family that the safest thing would be to take my secrets to the grave with me. But I will now take the risk and share as carefully as I can the hope that has been growing in my mind over the last twenty-eight years.

✳✳✳

First a few disclaimers. I do not hold to the concept of annihilation or "conditional immortality," as it has been called. This view says humans are not by nature immortal. When they trust in Jesus they receive the life that continues forever; with that they become immortal. Those who hold to this view may say that when unbelievers die that's their end. They die like animals. Or they may say unbelievers will be resurrected, judged, and then banished into total death forever. This view was strongly argued by Edward Fudge in 1982. Later the venerable evangelical statesman John R. W. Stott co-wrote a book that pleaded for the same. I've read them, as well as many of their current followers. I've listened to friends who hold this view. But I set the idea aside as having too little basis in Scripture, showing too little respect for the value of the total community of humankind, and displaying too little appreciation for the durable effectiveness of God's grace. The respected Croatian theologian Miroslav Volf argues that God's gracious creational plan is "unthinkable without continued life of human beings after death" (Polkinghorne, p. 277). Annihilation of human life looks too much like divine failure.

Further, I am not arguing for an unqualified universalism either. Universalism has been around since the early centuries of the church's history and is held by some modern theologians. It says the love of God will eventually overcome all evil and induce all humans to bow in trust before God. This would be wonderful if it would happen. However, I believe strongly in human free will, and I don't understand the strange mystery of human evil. How will people of unbelief think and behave and respond to God's grace in eternity? I don't know. God will not force his will on anybody. And I can't see any assurance in Scripture or reason that all *will* choose to repent and trust.

I was walking down a street in Oxford with Dr. Paul Fiddes who has been described as "one of Christianity's most distinguished scholars." We were discussing universalism versus particularism ("particularism" in this context refers to the New Testament doctrine that one receives salvation only through a particular faith in Jesus Christ). I suggested that a viable solution might be to keep the particular view that salvation is in Christ but then extend the opportunity for faith into eternity. Paul nodded approvingly and encouraged me to keep on working with the idea. That's what I'm doing here.

A friend who read this chapter wrote me, "But what if you are wrong?" That reminded me of a senior acquaintance in Oxford, John Wenham; he gave me an essay in which he passionately refutes the idea of endless torment in favor of eternal annihilation. At the end he adds, "I regard with utmost horror the possibility of being wrong." I understand him, but I don't shudder at the horror. I don't take myself *that* seriously. I face the question every time I stand up to preach, and I live with that because if we humans are called to proclaim the mysteries of God we are always liable to fall short. God will have to accept that. I would say I am utterly humbled by the profundity of what we are trying to do for God. I will try to be careful and prayerful about it. But the veracity will be judged by God, and with grace, I hope.

* * *

The hope I will now discuss is based on these five foundational convictions:

-Conscious existence, some form of living, continues beyond the grave for all humans.

-Those who trust in Jesus here are already living the eternal life of the future.

-God's grace and mercy has no end; it is as everlasting as God is.

-All will have an opportunity to meet Christ, if not in this life then after the grave, and to decide whether or not they will submit to the love of God.

-In spite of the infinite love of God, eternal lostness is a logical possibility because of the sacred gift of free choice that every person has received. Eternal separation from God will be a free choice, just as will eternal life with God.

Expanding on these basic principles, I will now enumerate the reasons why I hope for grace beyond the grave.

1. I hope because some of the most respected fathers of the early church believed the grace that invites sinners to repent will be functional beyond the grave. Clement of Alexandria (150-215), Origen (185-254), and Gregory of Nyssa (330-395), who used the same Scriptures we have today, believed the fire of the future is not punitive, but a purifying experience through which the deceased will progress on the way to salvation. Origen, who was a prolific writer and the most outspoken of the three, declared strongly that a temporary, remedial disciplining is more in line with God's mercy than eternal damnation. The views of these three were not universally accepted in their time. But the fact that learned men, at home in the Greek language and only a few centuries removed from their New Testament sources, could believe that references to hell should be understood figuratively must be taken seriously. See Jeffrey Trumbower's book for a recent study of the early materials; his sub-title is "The Posthumous Salvation of Non-Christians in Early Christianity." Of course, what the wise fathers of the past believed does

not *prove* anything, but it does tell me that the hope I have embraced is not a new-fangled, modernistic, liberal revision. Hope has been around!

It was Augustine (354-430) who firmly stamped out all hope in grace beyond the grave and declared the idea of posthumous salvation to be false. There is no grace after death, he said, because nothing changes after death. Augustine's theology was later dramatized by the Italian poet Dante (1265-1321). His three-part *Divine Comedy* provided the Medieval church with vivid, gruesome imaginations of the horrors of purgatory and hell. With these declarations these churchly wise men hung over the church a gloomy cloud from which it has not yet escaped.

2. I hope because of the "Probability Principle" to which a science teacher introduced me many years ago. I am not a "scientific" person, but this is how I remember him: Scientists don't need to prove their theories; they look at all sides of an issue, the pros and the cons, and then decide which explanation has the highest probability of being correct. He concluded proudly, "And using this "Probability Factor," we have recently sent a man to the moon.

Maybe current science teachers will laugh at my explanation above, but I have used the concept in my theology classes. Students like their teachers to have precise data; they want to think in white and black terms. They like to write essays with titles like "Three Factors that Prove God Is Real." And then I, killjoy professor that I am, would tell them no number of factors can *prove* God. Rather, we look at all the pointers, we explore all the evidences for one high God, and then we worship and believe and live on the basis of what is most likely true. It seems to me that all people with healthy minds think this way. They work with the Probability Factor when they choose what make of car to buy, where to invest their retirement money, and where to go on next winter's holidays. And I realize now that each chapter in this book developed around that principle.

Somewhere, the Oxford philosopher Richard Swinburne declared, "The idea of God is highly improbable, but the idea of no God is even more improbable." And so, he believed. In keeping with this principle, I will not try to *prove* that my interpretation is correct, but I will list the reasons why the concept of grace beyond the grave seems to integrate more neatly with the total body of biblical data than do the alternative theories.

3. Maybe my hope had its birth many years ago when I discovered this rule of interpretation: what is spoken or written figuratively must be understood figuratively. The Hebrew linguistic reservoir was chockfull of figurative concepts. Almost every sentence in the Psalms and the Prophets has a figurative detail or two. When this is not understood the most bizarre teachings can be pulled out of the Scriptures. Our first teachers told us to interpret everything as literally as possible. This is a recipe for error. In response to a question a teacher explained that if hell fire is figurative then the reality that it represents would have to be even *worse* than fire. I think that dismissive answer contains a logical fallacy. Rather, as carefully as we can we must understand what the writers meant to communicate with their terms and then interpret accordingly, whether literally or figuratively. This principle is especially important for our theme here because everything that pertains to the afterlife is completely beyond our personal experience, and is described figuratively in this-worldly terms and images. I will now illustrate that with a quick study of two terms that are crucial for the topic of salvation beyond the grave.

First, let's look at the word "fire." The ordinary, literal meaning is that it refers to what is going on in the firepot and cooks the food for supper (Isa. 64:2). But it can be used of God's punishment of bad people. The teacher I mentioned above seemed unaware of the wide metaphorical usage of "fire." It can be used of the troubles of life, as when Isaiah 43:2 says, "When you walk through fire you shall not be burned, and the flames shall not consume you." Human wickedness can be called "fire" (Isa. 9:18). The Lord's tongue is called a "devouring fire" (Isa. 30:27). And then the prophet's words are called a "devouring fire" (Jer. 5:14). In the New Testament the quality of a minister's work is tested by fire (1 Cor. 13-15). One's Christian faith may be tested by fire (1 Peter 1:7). Most fascinating and graphical of all is the language of 2 Peter 3:10-13, about the heaven's blazing and the elements melting with fire. This sounds as if all that will be left will be a smoky nuclear haze. But what does the apostle see? The fierce infernal scene results in "new heavens and a new earth, where righteousness is at home." A new world in which everything will be just right!

Now let's look at Jesus' "fire" language. Is he to be understood literally, or figuratively as in the passages above? Jesus made ten references to "Gehenna," which is described in Mark 9:48 as the place "where their worm never dies and the fire is never quenched." Most scholars say Gehenna was the name of Jerusalem's garbage dump. Some think it refers to a cite mentioned in Jeremiah as the place where abominable pagan rites, such as the sacrificing of children, were practiced. In either case, to the Jewish mind of that day, the term had only horrible connotations. Does it refer to the ultimate, eternal state of the unbeliever? Probably not. In most of the cases Jesus seems to be referring to the this-worldly alternative to joining the new kingdom he was starting up. Not submitting to the call of the kingdom would be like living on the garbage dump, among the worms and the smoldering fires. Horrible!

Now, let's look at the different meanings of "death" in the Bible. I've heard it emphasized that death means death. Death always refers to the end of life. Literally, it does. But figuratively it is used with other meanings.

Back in Genesis Adam was warned, "Be careful about that one tree; on the day you eat of that tree you will die" (Gen. 2:17). He ate, as his wife suggested, but he did not die that day. Genesis says he lived for hundreds of years after that day. What do we say to that? Probably the warning meant that the relationship of trust and intimacy for which he had been created would die.

Now I move ahead to the Gospel of John. John reports that Jesus invited people to join themselves to him in faith. Those who give themselves to Jesus in faith, step from death into life (John 5:24). In other words, those who don't trust Jesus are "dead." The letters of John use "death" in the same sense (1 John 3:14).

Paul usually follows the theology and language of John quite closely. He does the same with this theme. In Romans 8 he explains one can only live a just life with the help of the Spirit. Then he warns sharply, "To set the mind on the flesh is death but to set the mind on the Spirit is life and peace" (v. 6). In the Ephesian letter he reminds the readers that they once were *dead* in their trespasses and sins (2:1). The dead people in these verses had not been buried; they were still alive, but living apart from God.

The two words I've been following – "fire" and "death" – meet in Revelation 19, 20. Five times the "lake of fire" is mentioned. Not much is said about it, except that it is the "second death" (Rev. 20:14). The concept is hard to understand; some commentators don't even try. But let's try this: Maybe the state of separatedness from God, that started in Eden, that continued to be called death by John and Paul, continues after physical death, and is then, naturally, called the "second" death.

And maybe when Hebrews 12:29 says, "our God is a consuming fire," this may not mean that God destroys people but that God consumes sin and evil.

So now I suggest that the fire of eternity that is mentioned a few times in the Scriptures, may be a metaphor for the purging, purifying love of God, but it may seem like torment for those who resist the love.

And then I wonder, would it be too much to hope that the metaphorical fires that Peter saw renewing this physical world (2 Peter 3:12, 13) will also renew stubborn, proud, selfish people so that they will fit into the new world? I think Brian McLaren responds to this question with his tortuous theological fiction, *The Last Word and the Word After That*. The last word is hell, but after that there is the word of grace and forgiveness for all who choose to receive it. "Death" and "fire" are dark, ominous words, but they can be seen figuratively and then they allow me to hope.

I conclude this section with another word from George Macdonald, the Scottish minister and novelist who has the lofty romantic idea that hell is God's school for re-educating lost people. "Hell is God's and not the devil's. Hell is on the side of God and man, to free the child of God from the corruption of death" (p. 15).

4) I hope because there is nothing about the end of grace in the Bible. We don't read that at such and such a point God cannot or will not be gracious anymore. And since the Scriptures have no word, or even a hint, that grace will ever be withdrawn (Yes, I've checked all 159 cases of "grace" in the Bible), I think my hope is reasonable.

This is how it looks to me: The life without God that is called "Gehenna" in the Synoptics, that is called "death" in John and Paul, is at the end called the "second death." It is phase two, the eternal phase, of existing without God. It is this final lake of fire that theologians have in mind when they discuss hell as the state of ultimate lostness. Now, since anybody can at any stage in phase one turn to God in submission and faith, thereby stepping out of death to receive the gift of eternal life, I am hoping the opportunity will be there in phase two as well.

And then there is that beautiful Hebrew word *chesed.* It has such wonderful connotations that translators have hardly known what to do with it. The King James Bible called it "loving kindness." Some Bibles use "mercy." The NIV simply has the bland "love." The Bible I use translates it as "steadfast love." It is the key word that leads us to confidence in the constant goodness of God. Psalm 100:5 sums it up, "For the Lord is good, his steadfast love endures forever." That formulaic saying is used forty-one times in the Old Testament. Maybe we should take it seriously and believe it. *Chesed* is forever!

5) I am encouraged to hope when I read the Scriptures and notice the creative way in which God balances justice and mercy. We know that the Old Testament writings contain an abundance of material about God's severity. However, along with the incredible harshness there is a steady stream of love and compassion. It starts the first time God speaks about himself, "The LORD, a God merciful and gracious, slow to anger, and abounding in steadfast love and faithfulness" (Ex. 34:6).

The New Testament continues the witness to God's gracious compassion with the announcement that with the birth of the Savior, God is reaching out to make peace with the earth (Luke 2:14). John sees God's actions as an outreach of love, "God so loved the world that he gave his only Son." The entire body of Holy Scripture is presented against this backdrop of God's loving, relentless desire to bring his creation back into his arms. This produces an atmosphere of hope.

The simple prooftext support for my hope may be slim, but as Stephen Jonathan argues in a major study of grace beyond the grave, hoping for the dead is "theologically feasible" (p. xi). I will make it stronger; I suggest that trying to grasp the mystery of God's everlasting grace and love makes hope unavoidable for me. Professor Brian Hebblethwaite of Cambridge concludes, "In the light of the revealed nature of God, considerations of theodicy and of moral and religious plausibility encourage us to envisage further opportunities beyond the grave for men and women denied such opportunities on earth" (p. 218).

The dichotomy that some see between the justice and the mercy of God is false. God is totally just and totally merciful, all the time. However, neither is the same as human justice or mercy and we must not judge God by our standards. The Scriptures do not discuss either trait philosophically but both are shown functioning in God's relationship with his people.

Look at Abraham's encounter with his Lord in Genesis 18:16ff. The Lord tells Abraham he is going to destroy Sodom and Gomorrah. Abraham plants himself before the Lord and pleads, "You wouldn't destroy the cities if you find fifty good people there, would you? Shall not the Judge of all the earth do what is just?" Abraham talks him down, like an auction sale in reverse, until God promises that for ten righteous people he will spare the cities. I get the feeling the Lord was pleased that his human friend kept on appealing to his mercy.

My next illustration comes from Exodus 32-34. While Moses was with God on Mount Sinai the people convince brother Aaron to make a golden calf. They need a visible god whom they can honor for bringing them out of Egypt. God was horrified at this regressive display of pagan idolatry and announced he will consume them in his wrath and start a new community with Moses (32:10). Moses pleaded with God to remember the promises he had made in the past, and God changed his mind (32:14). God's encounters with Abraham and Moses both reveal that his announcement of destruction may conceal the unspoken provision of a possible reprieve from the doom.

Hosea 4 may be the most graphic and most damning picture of Israelite debauchery there is in the Bible. But even that is followed by these touching words of grace, "My heart recoils within me; my compassion grows warm and tender. I will not execute my fierce anger; I will not again destroy Ephraim; for I am God and no mortal, the holy one in your midst, I will not come in wrath" (11:8, 9).

In prophet after prophet the wrath that is announced at one point leads on to promises of mercy later on. The climax comes in Isaiah "For the mountains may depart and the hills be removed, but my steadfast love shall not depart from you, and my covenant of peace shall not be removed, says the Lord, who has compassion on you" (54:10).

And so I wonder, could God in the future be any less kind and gracious than he was in the past? Could God be any less hospitable than was the father in Jesus' timeless parable of the prodigal son, who turned from his hellish life with the pigs to accept the steadfast love of his father's embrace? I continue my wondering, could God be less forgiving than Jesus expects us to be when he demands that we reach out and forgive up to seventy times seven? Gerhard Lohfink wonders as well, "Can God, in the afterlife, treat history differently than in history itself, where God's true nature has been revealed in dialogue with God's people? . . . Can God act differently from the way, in human circumstances, every truly good parent acts toward his or her children?" (p. 158).

6. I hope because a constant theme in Scripture is that God will be glorified by the way he deals with his creation. The traditional view of hell that people have developed has beclouded his reputation. I suggest God will receive more honor and glory through the future repentance and salvation of those who have not known him here than by an endless inferno. The traditional view of hell seems like pure, endless retribution with no goal in sight.

7. I am moved towards hope when I read the writings of my professor friends in the "restorative justice" movement. They are convinced that it is possible to combine justice and mercy in a way that more effectively rehabilitates criminals and leads to a kinder and safer society than do the traditional methods of crime control that depend on retribution and punishment. I am quite convinced that God is even more creatively compassionate than our best restorative criminologists. Surely, what people can do God can do better.

8. I am greatly encouraged in my hoping for the dead when I notice how often the New Testament speaks of God's desire that *all* will be saved and that the Son visited this earth to make peace between God and *all* of humankind. I list here some of those key thoughts:

-Matthew 18:14: "It is not the will of your Father in heaven that one of these little ones should be lost."

-John 3:17: "God did not send the Son into the world to condemn the world, but in order that the world might be saved through him."

John 12:32: "And I . . . will draw all people to myself."

John 12:47: "I came not to judge the world, but to save the world."

Romans 5:18: ". . . One man's act of righteousness leads to justification and life for all."

Romans 11:32: "God has imprisoned all in disobedience so that he may be merciful to all."

1 Cor 15:22; "For as all die in Adam, so all will be made alive in Christ."

2 Cor 5:19: "In Christ God was reconciling the world to himself."

Ephesians 1:9, 10: "The mystery of his will . . . to gather up all things in him."

Philippians 2:10, 11: "At the name of Jesus every knee should bend . . . and every tongue should confess that Jesus Christ is Lord."

Colossians 1:20: "Through him God was pleased to reconcile all things to himself."

1 Timothy 2:3, 4: "God our Savior, who desires everyone to be saved."

1 Timothy 2:5, 6: "Christ Jesus, himself human, who gave himself a ransom for all."

1 Timothy 4:10: "... who is the Savior of all people, especially of those who believe."

Titus 2:11: "For the grace of God has appeared, bringing salvation to all."

2 Peter 3:9: "The Lord is . . . not wanting anyone to perish, but all to come to repentance."

1 John 2:2: "Jesus Christ . . . is the atoning sacrifice for our sins, and not for ours only but also for the sins of the whole world."

1 John 4:14: ". . . the Father has sent his Son as the Savior of the world."

Revelation 5:9: "By your blood you ransomed for God saints from every tribe and language and people and nation."

Revelation 22:17: "Let everyone who is thirsty come and . . . take the water of life as a gift."

These are my observations about the texts above:

-These references are spread quite uniformly over the entire New Testament.

-We notice that often the object of God's saving work is mentioned inclusively as "all" or "the world."

-God's saving work is always done through Christ.

-I am aware that interpreters can qualify some of these statements, so that they don't mean what they seem to say, but I suggest that the cumulative weight of these lines cannot easily be explained away.

-The general emphasis here and throughout all Scripture is that God's desire and offer to save always calls for a voluntary, personal response. I expect this will be true in eternity as well.

-None of these hopeful statements is given a time limit, that is, there is no suggestion that God's saving love is limited to the present earthly time.

-Since God desires all to be saved and since Jesus died for all, it would seem strange if God would not give everybody the chance to meet Jesus and decide about him.

9. I keep on hoping even though the Scriptures do not speak directly of salvation beyond the grave. However, I notice hints that invite me to hope. On one occasion Jesus was responding to those who accused him of having healing powers because he was possessed by Satan, the demon king (Matt. 12:22-32). He said that making accusations like that against the Son of Man is forgivable. But speaking against the Holy Spirit is never forgivable, not now or *in the age to come*. This sounds as if God's grace of forgiveness will be functioning in the next age as well as here.

When the apostle Paul was summing up the end-time events for the believers in Thessalonica he spoke of "our Lord Jesus Christ, who died for us, so that whether we are awake or asleep we may live together with him (1 Thess. 5:10). Commentators usually say that the sleepers are those who have already died, as in 4:14 (NIV). However, the Greek word for "sleep" in this sentence is not the word he used in 4:14. It is the word he used in 5:6, 7 of those who are *spiritually* asleep. In other words, he seems to say that both, those who are spiritually alert and those who are spiritually indifferent have a potential future with Christ.

In 1 Peter 3:18, 19 the apostle Peter says that after his death Jesus was "made alive in the spirit, in which also he went and made proclamation to the spirits in prison." This raises many questions. Did Jesus do this after his resurrection or did he do it in spirit form before the resurrection? Who, or what, are the spirits in prison? What is this spirit prison? What was the purpose of the preaching? Did this give the imprisoned spirits an opportunity to trust in Jesus? Are some of our questions answered in 4:6? "For this is the reason the gospel was proclaimed even to the dead, so that, though they had been judged as everyone is judged, they might live in the spirit as God does." Most interpreters deal cautiously with this text.

However, William Barclay is not quite as inhibited as most are and offers this comment, "Peter has this amazing idea that Christ descended to the world of the dead and preached the gospel there, and that very fact means that even though they had been judged by death, the dead had still another chance to grasp the gospel and live in the spirit of God" (p. 295). The Swedish scholar Bo Reicke agrees, but more cautiously, "Thus it seems to be a question of dead people . . . who hear the gospel in Hades, in order to be judged in the last day in the flesh, and to live in the Spirit" (p. 206). In my study guide on Peter's letters (2009) I skirted the controversies, as most commentators do. But today, trying to grasp the intention of the two passages, I see more credibility in Barclay and Reicke than I was willing to grant then.

Finally, Hebrews 7:24 mentions Christ's eternal priesthood and then assures us, "Consequently he is able for all time to save those who approach God through him, since he always lives to make intercession for them."

10. To everything I've said above I add another reason why I hope – I read theologians who advocate the thesis that death finally provides the person with the opportunity to choose, in unimpeded and complete freedom, for or against God. That hope is teasingly, enticingly waved in front of us in Revelation 21, the second last chapter in the Bible.

Let's now walk through that chapter. All of Revelation is couched in vivid, apocalyptic, figurative imagery. The images show us what heaven is like, what the Roman Empire is like, and what the invisible powers of evil are like. It reveals what is going on behind the visible earthly happenings, that the kingdom of the devil is inspiring the Roman Empire to oppose the gracious saving work of the Holy Trinity. Often the scenes are dark, troubling, and ominous. As one reads one may wonder, which power is finally going to win this cosmic conflict for the loyalty of humankind.

And then at 21:1 the picture suddenly changes. On the screen before us we see the new heaven and new earth. We assume this is the same heaven and earth that Peter was waiting for, in which righteousness will be at home (2 Peter 3:13). The loud voice that has frequently been shouting the good news throughout Revelation announces, "The first things have passed away." This may refer to the visions with which

Chapters 19 and 20 concluded, which have shown that all that opposes or contradicts the will of God is dumped into the lake of fire (19:20; 20:10; 20:14, 15).

Then John saw the holy city, the new Jerusalem, coming down from God. This is the goal, the climax, the fantastic termination of the ghastly, gory, satanic uprising that has tried to wreck God's plan for his creation throughout the earthly era.

Then, after John has heard the voice announcing what it will be like in this new world (21:3-8), he is shown a second vision of the new world. This is common in Revelation; a vision may be followed by a second picture of the same, but from a different perspective. For example, we see six (some scholars see seven) depictions of the end of the world as the drama unfolds. Here, the second vision informs us what the descending city represents. One of the attending angels explains, "Come, I will show you the bride, the wife of the Lamb" (21:9). That is followed by another report of the holy city descending from God. Every Christian reader in 95 AD would have understood that the city represents the church. This is the eternal community of those who, through trust and loyalty, have been received into the church of Jesus Christ. The multitude before the throne, that could not be counted in chapter 7, is here a city. Of all the apocalyptic visions of Revelation this is actually one of the easiest to understand. This is not *where* the bride lives, this *is* the bride. A pastor to whom I once explained this said, "You mean you take it that literally?" Yes, I accept the angel's words as literal truth, that the amazing city that comes out of the sky is a figurative vision of the church of Jesus Christ. This is the future glory of that hymn-singing bunch of losers who were being fed to the lions in Rome every day.

My students would ask why are the physical details so specific if it actually speaks of people. I have a few ideas about that. First, Jesus started it in Matt. 16:18, "On this rock I will build my church." Here in Revelation is the consummation of the construction project Jesus announced there. Next, I read that Paul said to the church in Corinth, "You are God's building" (1 Cor. 3:9). Then he explains that he has laid the foundation, which is Jesus Christ, and others are now building upon it. In Ephesians 2:20-22 he writes that the one unified church has been built upon the foundation of the apostles and prophets, and the whole structure is now growing together to become a holy temple in the Lord.

Peter understands the same concept; his readers are advised, "Like living stones, let yourselves be built into a spiritual house" (1 Peter 2:5). The people who had these Scriptures will have found the imagery of Revelation quite understandable.

I said Revelation teases and tantalizes us with a series of fascinating pictures of the glorified church in eternity. Here is what we see in verses 22-27: First, there is no temple in the city, because the Lord God and the Lamb (Jesus Christ) are directly present (Temples used to represent the invisible God). There will be no need for the sun or moon because the glory of the Lord will be its light. There will be no night, which probably means no sin, ignorance, confusion, or deception. The kings and their people will bring the glory of the nations into it. And the gates will never be shut, which suggests that the doors of the church are always open.

Now, notice that even though the kings and the people will enter, only those are entering whose names are written in the Lamb's book of life. This suggests to me that even in eternity there will be the opportunity to sign up for Jesus, and there may be those who don't. All twelve gates of the majestic city stand open to welcome them if they do. Evangelists have preached that when Christ comes the doors will be shut forever; here at the end of the New Testament they stand open forever!!!

And so, I start dreaming. I am not dogmatizing or declaring how it will be. But I believe the evidence I have accumulated allows me to dream in hope. I dream that maybe those millions of people who lived and died before the Savior appeared may have a chance to meet the Savior in eternity and then qualify to enter the city.

I dream that those people who never believed in Jesus because the missionaries never got there may hear the gospel in eternity.

I dream that those missionaries who have toiled all their lives and have seen almost no results may see people, who were too weak or scared or confused, or too bound up by their traditions to submit to Jesus in their traditional social settings, finally find the freedom to choose for Jesus there.

I dream that some people who have been sincerely devoted to deities with other names may realize their error in eternity and there recognize Jesus Christ as the truth they always were seeking.

I dream that those Christians who have generations of deceased relatives who never heard the gospel may there see them, responding to a love they never understood, streaming in through those open doors to join them in the heavenly church.

I dream that some of the youth I have known who lived carelessly and thoughtlessly and then died instantly will come to their senses in eternity and surrender there to Jesus.

I dream that the woman who turned against the church and the Lord because she once was seduced and raped by a minister of the church will in heaven receive the grace to look past that evil and say yes to Jesus.

Would it surprise you if the God who loves the whole world would have such a plan and such a compassion? Do you imagine God is less compassionate than you or I would be if we would decide on the eternal fate of our neighbors? As Abraham once put it, "Shall not the God of all the earth do right?" I expect he will. That gives me the hope to keep on expecting the best.

To conclude this chapter I go to the evangelical theologian Gabriel Fackre who concludes his history of God and creation with these words, "Christians have a right *to hope* that eternal death means the burning love of an eternal God cleansing the dross as only eternity can do" (p. 227). He adds that this is a modest hope, "leaving all to God's final mysterious Purpose." To this hope I add the caution of the Eastern Orthodox theologian Timothy Ware, "It is heretical to say that all *must* be saved, for this is to deny free will; but it is legitimate to hope that all *may* be saved" (Nichols, p. 181).

### For Further Thought and Study

*1. What problems do you have when you try to integrate the traditional concept of hell into a Christian worldview?*

*2. What is the biblical or theological basis for believing that death is final and that there will be no grace after that?*

*3. How comfortable are you with the suggestion that God's loving desire to win humans back to himself may continue after earthly death?*

*4. How can we integrate the biblical pictures of God's severity with the repeated assurances that we can count on God's compassion, mercy, and grace?*

*5. Read Matthew 25:31-46. What was the main lesson Jesus wanted to teach his disciples with this parabolic picture? How could the suggestion that post-judgment fire is for correction and reform fit into this passage?*

*6. Read 1 Peter 3:18-22 and compare with 4:5,6. What do you conclude?*

*7. What do you conclude from the list of references above that speak of God's desire to save all?*

*8. Read Revelation 21:22-27 and let your imagination run with it. What does this suggest to you about the church of Christ in eternity?*

# Chapter 11. Hope That the Kingdom Will Come

*We are living 'between the times' – between the time when Jesus introduced God's new era and the time when he will return to establish God's kingdom in its final form.* – Stephen Travis

*The Spirit is the eschatological power by which the present age will be transformed into the kingdom of God.* – Ted Peters

*The end of the story is not destruction, not even the end of the world. The end is the fulfillment of God's promises and the restoration of God's reign of justice and mercy forever.* – David Tiede

*Jesus . . . must remain in heaven until the time of universal restoration that God announced long ago through his holy prophets* (Acts 3:20, 21).

*For I am about to create new heavens and a new earth; the former things shall not be remembered or come to mind* (Isaiah 65:17).

In Chapter 8, discussing the troubles of this life, I spoke of the hope that at the end all things will be well. That chapter spoke of personal troubles. Now we take the bigger, comprehensive view, which is that we can count on God to look after his world and bring it all, the visible and the invisible, to a beautiful conclusion.

I continue with the idea, already expressed in Chapter 10, that God may culminate this earthly human project more gracefully than we have dared to expect. Frederick Farrar suggests that Mariolatry, the prayerful worship of the Virgin Mary, was attractive to medieval believers because their concept of God was too grim and severe. A God who functioned as the "Eternal Torturer" seemed unapproachable. In our time many thoughtful believers find it hard to fathom that a God who joyfully created an incredibly beautiful universe as an expression of love (Prov. 8:22-31) will finally decide to destroy it all in fiery fury. This chapter proposes a hopeful alternative to such dark views of God's sovereignty.

The Pauline assurance is that God "is able to accomplish far more than all we can ask or imagine" (Eph. 3:20). Is that just a sweet comforting sentiment, like a Hallmark wish, or a principle that we can apply to the deepest needs of our existence? J. H. Leckie writes that "Christian faith in all ages has cherished a secret hope richer and more tender than it has been able to express" (p. 290). I think I understand. I also have sensed around me a deep unspoken hope that maybe the eternal future will turn out better than our commitment to orthodox theology allows us to expect. What many long for I will here try to put into simple words.

I write with the conviction that the Bible is not a textbook of religious dogma. It is not a manual that tells us what to believe. It is a record of historical events that we use to form our dogmas. It is relatively easy to select from its materials individual statements that can be interpreted very darkly. We can use biblical verses to build a case for a mean, resentful, violent God. On the other hand, we can focus on the love that God has shown to the world in the person of Jesus. If we work with the view that Jesus came because God loves the world, that God would rather save humans than damn them, it seems difficult to believe that God will simply banish all unbelievers to everlasting fiery torment simply because they have not heard about Jesus or because social factors made it impossible for them to believe. And it seems difficult to understand why this earth has to be destroyed to make way for an eternal home for the true believers. So, my question is, can we put aside the idea of God as the "Angry Exterminator" and see God rather as the "Great Lover" who steadfastly pursues his beloved?

Before we look at the big themes that should direct our thinking about the future of this world I will reflect on the occasional touches of sparkling, teasing good news that flash at us, here and there, out of the text of Scriptures. Martin Luther once had such a flash of inspiration when he read about "the earnest expectation of the creature" in Romans 8:19 (Moltmann, *Theology of Hope,* p. 35). My flash of inspiring hope came when I read Acts 3:21 (to be discussed later). Moltmann speaks of these flashes as glimpses of the creative, inventive imagination of God's love. We can't exactly place our finger on it, it's hard to see how the visions of the future will fit into this earthly framework. However, the "passion for the possible," as Kierkegaard called it, beckons us on to the bright promises of the future. Moltmann laments the fact that this visionary hope has been more acceptable in the Christianity of the fanatics than in the establishments of the Christian church.

Now we move to the big, basic concepts. There is the idea that a new revolutionary kingdom has invaded, or intruded into, this world. The powers of this world have been confronted and challenged by a heavenly visitation. I am speaking of the appearing of Jesus, the Messiah. Many of us pray regularly as Jesus taught us to pray, "May your kingdom come; may your will be done on earth as it is in heaven" (Matt. 6:10). The kingdom had arrived (Matt. 12:28), right into the heart of Jewish Palestine. The goal was that it would spread out to the whole world and transform it to resemble heaven. This is the "coming" for which the disciples of Jesus are to pray.

The kingdom was present in the person of Jesus. Jesus was, humanly speaking, a Jew among Jewish people. But he came to the Jewish people to save the world. The Jewish people, the family of Abraham, had been elected to be a witness to the world, to be the channel of truth from God to the world. In Jesus Christ this original plan (Gen. 12:3) reached its point of fulfillment.

The hope that God will ultimately fix up everything that is wrong flashed into *my* mind when I read Acts 3:21. My religious culture had taught me to think of God as the eschatological destroyer, who will eventually burn up this contaminated earth and banish all evil spirits and all unbelievers to the eternal lake of fire. The idea that God might have a way to fix things up was foreign to me. But in Acts 3 Peter is standing on the temple steps, in Jerusalem, and he is preaching. He reminds them that a few weeks ago they killed Jesus. Jesus who? The Holy and Righteous One, the Author of life. Imagine: they, the citizens of the holy city, murdered the One who invented life. How paradoxical can it get? But the Almighty Creator snubbed his nose at those defenders of the traditional faith. He raised to life the one whom they had killed; they wanted him dead, God wanted him alive. You see, death is not God's thing; he is the living God who created all of earthly life.

Those events in Jerusalem were a demonstration of truth; there humankind hit the bottom of its long, ugly slide into ungodliness; there God shows what he thinks of this world's death culture. The disciples there picked up the idea that if God can raise the dead then dying is no big deal anymore. There they recognized that if God can raise the dead then he can fix everything else as well. Peter challenged the listeners to repent and turn to God so that God might send them their Messiah. However, he cautioned that the Messiah would remain in heaven "until the time of universal restoration" (Acts 3:21); this was my startling, illuminating thought. N. T. Wright refers to the variety of theological opinions that were stewing in the theological milieu of first century Judaism. But, on one point there was agreement. "They all believed in the hope of Israel – the hope for a great divine rescue" (*Paul*, p. 138). That was what they would have heard in Peter's words. The important word is *apokatastasis*. My Arndt & Gingrich Greek Lexicon says the term refers to "the time for restoring everything to perfection." Peter says this hope was announced long ago by the holy prophets. Instead of trying to work my way through the prophets I list here, for your study, some of the things the *apostles* had to say about this hope: 1 Corinthians 15:24-28; 2 Corinthians 5:19; Ephesians 1:9, 10; Philippians 2:10, 11; Colossians 1:19, 20; Revelation 1:17, 18; 11:15; 22:3, 4.

However, the most important words on our theme are those that lit up Luther's mind, Romans 8:18-25. Here is the core part of the passage:

> For the creation waits with eager longing for the revealing of the children of God; for the creation was subjected to futility,
> not of its own will but by the will of the one who subjected it, in hope that creation itself will be set free from its bondage to decay and will obtain the freedom of the glory of the children of God. We know that the whole creation has been groaning in labor pains until now, and not only the creation, but we ourselves, who have the first fruits of the Spirit, groan inwardly while we wait for adoption, the redemption of our bodies.

The apostle personifies creation and says all of creation has been waiting, longing, and groaning to be set free from its bondage to corruption and decay. This painful anticipation is shared by humans who have received the Spirit. Not only are believers waiting to be redeemed from their earthiness, but their entire natural environment will, hopefully, be changed with them. We wish the hope would have more specific details.

But the terseness is no reason to ignore these words. What is clear is that instead of a global holocaust that will exterminate everything, which is what many believers have expected, there will be a universal renewal. These are God's words of promise and we accept them with the assurance that the God who is the Father of our Lord has the authority and the power to bring about his promises, regardless of how implausible they may seem to us.

\* \* \*

Jesus' "kingdom of God" idea needs further explication. It is evident to anyone who reads the Bible that there is more to God's world than what we see around us. There seem to be two kinds of "stuff." Over the years I have used different terms for this duality, but in recent years I have adopted N. T. Wright's terminology, that our worldview must recognize two "dimensions" of reality. First of all, there is the reality with which we have direct experience. This is the world that scientists explore with microscopes or telescopes and which we can observe. This is *our* world. This is the entire physical universe. We belong to it. This is the world of time and matter. Everything that we can see, explore, and examine, from minute sub-atomic particles to the billions of galaxies, each with their billions of stars, extending out into the immeasurable distance, is this world. In the middle of it (as we like to think) is our earth, one tiny speck of rock and earth with its incredible greenery, living growth, and the fascinating array of living creatures. And then there are we, over seven billion of us at this point, individual, unique, different human beings. This is what we will call the first dimension.

Then there is the second dimension. This other world, as far as we can understand, is not bound by the principles of physics that rule the first dimension. It could not be controlled by physical principles because it is not physical or temporal. It is immaterial and eternal. At home in the second dimension is the triune Creator, who is responsible for the first dimension. Also, to the second dimension belong the angels, the bad spirits, the devil, the state of heaven and the state of hell. There can be inter-communication between the two realms. In the first place, we know about the other dimension only because we have been hearing from there. Words of truth have been coming from there to here, from God to us.

Humans in the first dimension are invited to pray to God in the eternal dimension; we are assured that he hears and pays fatherly attention to all sincere praying. Throughout the history that the Bible reports, and in the folk stories of many different religious and ethnic groups, there are stories of angels who have visited here with messages from the other world. In fact, a Norwegian theologian has written a book about the world-wide phenomenon of angels and uses this as a way to argue for the existence of God (Peter Williams, *The Case for Angels*).

And then there is the report that the Christ has been here; he came from the eternal, spiritual dimension to spend some time, as a physical person, with us in this physical world. The divine purpose of his visit was to begin a revolution, the process of transformation that would bring the entire world with its people back into line with God's will. It was like a foreign kingdom invading this world and establishing a beachhead here in preparation for further conquest. It is probably called a kingdom because the prophets of the past, living and speaking within the milieu of the striving, struggling kingdoms of the Middle East, found it meaningful to speak of God's work as another kingdom. Isaiah speaks of it figuratively, as a mountain that will be set up among the nations of the world (2:2-4). The Psalmists frequently referred to three aspects of God's kingly rule: God is *king* (Ps. 10:16), there is a *kingdom* of God (Ps. 22:28), God *reigns* over his world (Ps. 96:10). With his kingdom language Jesus identified his presence with that Old Testament witness. Further, he called it the kingdom of *God* because through him the influence and power of God was at work in the world. In Matthew's Gospel it is called the kingdom of *heaven* because Jesus came to introduce the values of heaven, the values of the other dimension, into this earthly dimension. When Jesus taught us to hope for, and pray, that the kingdom would come he meant that it was to come to the world and not stay resident and localized in little Palestine.

I suggest that one cannot make sense of the Bible's message of hope unless one can somehow incorporate Jesus' kingdom thinking into our worldview. What we hope for is that in some way the kingdom of heaven will be integrated into the kingdom of this world. Currently the two are still badly at odds with each other. The book of Revelation was written to dramatize this earthly conflict between the two powers. It informed the late first century church that the idolatry that the Empire was trying to impose upon the church was the visible, sensory expression of a bitter battle being waged in the unseen spiritual dimension.

Revelation pictures it as a battle for the loyalty of humankind. It's the confrontation between truth and error. The Empire is based on deception and falsehood. Jesus visited this kingdom of deadly untruth to bear witness to the kingdom of truth. That's how he put it when he was on trial before Pontius Pilate, the agent of the Empire (John 18:36-38). But the strong man who represented Rome had no use for truth. Rome was built on dominating power, not truth. He decided that in the interests of Rome's stake in his far eastern province this troublesome messenger of truth might as well be executed. Rome did not need truth!

Revelation presents the battle for the loyalty of people mostly with images of brutal, murderous warfare. Some readers miss the point of the drama in their search for spiritual blessings in the text. Some abhor the violence so strongly that they refuse to read or study the book. But it is clear that in this chaotic violence, in a war in which the people of Jesus seem to be hopeless weaklings, the Lord Jesus is already reigning. Suddenly, in the midst of the bloody mayhem, the shout is heard, "The kingdom of the world has become the kingdom of our Lord and of his Messiah" (Rev. 11:15). David Tiede comments, "The immediate future was dire . . . . But the victory had already been declared" (p. 88).

At the center of our hope for the eventual victory of the kingdom of God over its seditious enemy is the resurrection of Jesus. I follow the thinking of 1 Corinthians 15 here. In the resurrection of Jesus the intangible hope of the Christian was made physically visible. Lots of people saw him alive after he had been killed (v.3-9). The apostle goes on to explain that not only is there no salvation without the resurrection of Christ, not only is Christ's resurrection a model for our future, but it is a promise of how all of creation will be rescued from its condemnation to death. Here the hints of hope we saw in Romans 8:19-25 are fleshed out. What God did with the human, physical Jesus after death had taken him away is a preview of what God promises to do with all of creation. This was the plan, the aim, the goal of the entire incarnational outreach of love for the world. The world was not destined for destruction, but for redemption through the relentless love of God.

\* \* \*

At this point some readers may wonder how current environmental alarms fit into God's scheme of things. Will we with our flagrant polluting destroy the world that God wants to redeem? How does the environmental Armageddon that has recently been predicted for 2030 relate to God's future? Are we perhaps messing this world up so badly that Christ will have to come back very soon to rescue us from the impending doom? I don't know! I thank God often for our comfortable lifestyle. But I also admit that I'm deeply concerned about the ecological consequences of our easy life. For me, the problem seems beyond any remedy. And I find no specific connection to this modern dilemma in the futurism of the Bible.

In response to this unwelcome subject some biblical believers may wonder why we even bother or fuss about cleaning up the earth. If we believe God will eventually, somehow, bring in his kingdom to transform the world why should we worry or be agitated? Is God concerned about such temporal matters? Is the problem worthy of prayerful attention?

It seems to me that believers who hope for the full coming of God's kingdom should, of all people, be most concerned about treating this present world with respect. God thinks this world is worth saving. We should agree with God and learn to think about the world as he does. In the kingdom that we are anticipating the will of God will be done perfectly. We believe that the kingdom of God has already broken into history. Consequently, those who profess allegiance to the new kingdom should do all they can to make God's will a reality now. If we pray as Jesus taught us to pray we should also see ourselves as the instruments to make it happen. If we long sincerely for the new heavenly principles of peace, love, and justice to take effect now we should do all we can to promote them in our areas of influence. God's promises for the future do not make our responsibility to care about the earth redundant. Our trust in God's long-range plan should lead to creative action and a joyful expression of love for God's earth. Stephen Travis reminds us that as we commit ourselves to be God's agents of the new way "we are pointing to the nature of God's final kingdom" (p.118).

The Christ who has been raised will rule over this tormented world of suffering people until all that is out of sync with God's will is going to be gone (1 Cor. 15:20-28). Christ will actively reign, even if invisibly behind the scenes, until all enemy resistance has been overcome. The last enemy to be vanquished is death (v. 26). When all is said and done and all the bad stuff is gone, when God has finished what he started here in Jesus, even death will be a thing of the past. Then Christ will hand his kingdom over to God the Father "so that God may be all in all." That is our hope!

\* \* \*

The hope that we are studying in this chapter sometimes sounds as if God will do a new work of creation. Four times the Scriptures speak of the future appearance of new heavens and a new earth (Isa. 65:17, 66:22, 1 Peter 3:13, Rev. 21:1). The Bible's use of "heaven" has caused confusion. People have wondered, "Why does heaven need to be made new? We thought heaven was perfect." It helps to realize that the word "heaven" refers many times in Scripture to the visible sky above us. When we look up and see the blue expanse that is heaven. When the writers needed a word for the eternal world of the future, the dimension in which God resides, they used the same word "heaven." The four texts cited do not speak about the heavenly home of eternity. They simply agree that the entire *physical* universe, earth and sky and all that is included, will in some way be recreated.

The 2 Peter passage is especially significant for us here. Peter remembers the destructive flood story of Noah's time. Ultimately God will again deal with all that is wrong in his world. However, God will keep the promise he gave to the world in Noah's day; he will never again destroy by a flood (Gen. 9). This time he will use fire, Peter says. But notice, the fire does not represent destruction, but a transformative purification. The result of the fire is not no earth, not ashes and a smoky nuclear haze, but a new earth in which righteousness is at home. Righteousness will be entrenched in this new world of the future; in other words, in this new world all things will be right.

Peter's vision of the future illustrates a point I have made earlier, that images of calamitous fire can be used, not to predict destruction and extermination, but cleansing and renewal. God's redemptive work is a process of recreation. The old is not destroyed, it is not discarded as garbage, but transformed into the new that will fit into the framework of the new world in its eternal spiritual dimension. David Tiede concludes, "The end of the story is not destruction, not even the end of the world. The end is the fulfillment of God's promises and the restoration of God's reign of justice and mercy forever" (p. 92).

God's redemptive work is a process of recreation. This will involve the bringing together, the complete integration of the two dimensions of reality. In Revelation this point is reached when the one on the throne announces, "See, I am making all things new" (21:5). Ted Grimsrud adds the important reminder that God will not make new *things*, he will take the things that are and make *them* new (p. 163).

This theme of eventual restoration would not be complete without reference to the judgment to come. God does not simply ignore sin. In John 5 Jesus presents himself as the judge of all people; he has received this authority from the Father. The current reign of Christ (1 Cor. 15:25) should probably be understood as the reign of judgment. There is judgment going on constantly as we live out our lives in the presence of God. And then there will be judgment on the other side of death, which means, judgment in the eternal, spiritual dimension. Christ is with us now as judge and he will render final judgment at the end. The Scriptural references to judgment do not say much about the penalties that will be inflicted or how past injustices will be rectified, except that there will be rewards, punishment, and fire. Since the final judgments will be in the eternal era, it is not surprising that they seem mysterious to us now.

We should not expect that the Judge will in eternity force people to love him (if such were even possible) or that he will demand or enforce allegiance, such as earthly dictators often do. While we may not understand eternal justice, we should accept the Pauline conviction that we will reap whatever we have been sowing (Gal. 6:7).

I find it strange that the biblical theme of judgment has often been seen as bad news and has been used mainly to frighten people about the future. The reminders about the judgment to come do not annul the effects of God's forgiving grace. Sin that has been forgiven cannot be judged. They are not remembered (Heb. 10:17). In the middle of Jesus' teaching on judgment he inserts, "Very truly, I tell you, everyone who hears my word and believes him who sent me has eternal life, and does not come under judgment, but has passed from death to life" (John 5:24). If these people of "life" will face a court of law in eternity they will hear only the happy announcement of forgiveness (Rom. 8:31-34).

A second problem is that we tend to see judgment only as a procedure to dig up what we had hoped would stay buried. Jesus' words in Luke 8:17 have unsettled us, "for nothing is hidden that shall not be disclosed, nor is anything secret that will not become known and come to light." We read that and we shudder with apprehension. But wait a minute; that may mean that all the good deeds, all the injustices we have endured, all the sacrifices we have made for others and have never been recognized, will come to light. I expect many will in eternity receive a much kinder judgment than they have received here from the neighbors or their peers or even from their church. Let's discard the idea that sees God only as the universal criminal judge whose job is to dig up as much dirt as possible. To balance this up I add Jurgen Moltmann's eloquent words (*Sun of Righteousness,* p. 135):

> God's supreme justice will 'create' justice for the victims of wickedness, will raise them up out of the dust, will heal their wounded lives, and put to rights the lives that have been destroyed. The victims wait for God's creative justice, which will bring them liberty, health and new life.

This about sums it up. This is what's going on. This is our hope. Maybe we are half ways there; maybe we are 99% of the way to the ultimate consummation. The promise is based on the fact that Christ has been here to get the project rolling and that he's coming back to finish it. God is planning to fix this mess, to clean up all the residue of human evil, to straighten out all the crookedness, and wipe away all traces of the enemy's malicious intentions. The day is coming when there will be no more killing and no more dying. There will be life! This world will be the kind of world in which Father, Son, and Spirit will be perfectly at home. To this I add Tiede's conclusion (p. 95):

> And this vision of the future has persisted since the New Testament era. It has been co-opted by empires, twisted into personal programs of success, and systematized into charts and predictions. But at its heart and in its historical origins, the future that Jesus announced is not subject to such control or manipulation. It comes by faith in the God of Israel who keeps promises. This future and its security are a gift.

And then there is the vision of Miroslav Volf, that the eternal kingdom will be "undiluted enjoyment of God, of one another, and of their environment, in a new world of perfect love" (Polkinghorne, p. 277).

## For Further Thought and Study

*1. After reading the first few paragraphs, how would you describe your concept of the future of the world?*

*2. Kierkegaard said a cosmic hope has been more acceptable to religious fanatics than to the established church. Why is that?*

*3. What difficulties do you have connecting Jesus' kingdom teaching with the future restoration of the world?*

*4. Read through the list of references that speak of God's future work and then read Romans 8. What do you conclude?*

*5. Consider the three options: God will destroy everything, human pollution will ruin everything, God will renew it all. Which is most likely? Why?*

*6. If God will use his creative word to renew all things, why are we supposed to pray and work that it may happen?*
*7. What are the problems with seeing references to God's fierce fire as a metaphor for his restorative work?*

*8. What will it take for you to recognize judgment as good news (Rom. 2:16)?*

# 12. The Hope of Heaven

*The Bible shows the way to go to heaven, not the way the heavens go.* – Galileo Galilei

*Ah, but a man's reach should exceed his grasp, or what's a heaven for.* – Robert Browning

*The love of heaven makes one heavenly.* – William Shakespeare

*But our citizenship is in heaven, and it is from there that we are expecting a Savior, the Lord Jesus Christ* (Phil. 3:20).

*For we know that if the earthly tent we live in is destroyed, we have a building from God, a house not made with hands, eternal in the heavens* (2 Cor. 5:1).

In December of 2002 I was preparing to preach at the funeral of a good friend, when I opened that Saturday's issue of *The Globe and Mail*. A whole section was devoted to death and funerals. Eight essays and six smaller sidebars. I read them eagerly, hoping to find some fresh ideas to brighten up my thinking that had become dull and uncreative from a wearying rash of too many funerals. What did I find? One mention of God, one sarcastic reference to the resurrection, and one mention of peace. Nothing about hope, heaven, or the fact that some people expect to live even though they die. Obviously, I concluded, the secular worldview is suffering from a worse inspirational drought than I am, so I returned to my Bible.

When we explore the concept of heaven we are dealing with an aspect of the eternal dimension. In order to help you follow my thinking I need to explain something about time and eternity. I assume that since God created a world that would function in time, the eternal God is now with us in time as well. I have written about the eventual integration of this temporal earthly dimension with the eternal, spiritual dimension. This means that the thoughts that I think and write assume a future, not of timeless eternity but of eternal time. I've been gratified to notice that more and more recent scholars have seen the eternal future this way. I'm thinking, for example, of philosopher William Lane Craig of California and theologian Brian Hebblethwaite of Cambridge. The latter insists that the final consummation of all things cannot be thought of in "non-temporal terms" (p. 207). In other words, we cannot have eternity without time because things keep on happening in eternity. We are not anticipating a static state of eternal nothingness, but an ongoing life of growth, change, and worship. It is the concept of eternal time that provides us with the framework for postulating that there will be opportunities for growth and development beyond the grave.

My discussion of heaven begins with Hebblethwaite's conclusion, that the "state of ultimate perfection must involve an endlessly dynamic movement of experience, ecstasy, exploration and activity (though one hopes for some rest as well!" (p. 207). That conviction, I believe, coheres beautifully with what I have been finding in the Bible and have been developing here over the previous chapters.

First, we have to revisit the prospect of the resurrection. It will not involve the restoration of old stuff that has decayed, nor will it require a new kind of *physical* stuff. It will be the recreation of stuff that is spiritual. And if my suggestions in Chapter 9 are correct, it happens at the point of death. As I've explained at funerals, the hope of resurrection does not require that we imagine new bodies popping out of the cemetery sod. We will be raised not as the same old physical people, but as new persons designed for another world. If we want to use the "body" word, to give more substance to the hope, we will have to follow Paul's example and refer to them as "spiritual bodies" (1 Cor. 15:44), whatever they are. Paul doesn't even *try* to tell us. He just points to the resurrected Jesus as one visible example of them (1 Cor. 15:45-49). If this all sounds confusing, let's just say that we will live after we die. Where? In heaven!

Heaven is the end state, the ultimate consummation, of the process of creation. As I explained in the previous chapter, studying the biblical theme of heaven has led to some major confusions. The Hebrew word *shamayim* and the Greek *ouranos* have the same meanings. Both can be used of the sky above us; often it just means "up there." Both Testaments also use heaven to identify the God we worship. Jonah confessed that his Jahweh was the God of heaven (Jon. 1:9). The same is often said of God in the New Testament, as in the well-known, "Our Father in Heaven" (Matt. 6:9). The "heaven" term is widely used in the New Testament. There are many references to the angels of heaven (Matt. 18:10), of Jesus having come from heaven (John 6:38), of the rewards laid up in heaven (Luke 6:23) and about storing up treasures in heaven (Mat. 6:20). But there is no direct mention of humans going to heaven or of being taken to heaven. How then has the doctrine of heaven become a major plank in the hope of the church? By a number of suggestive pointers that tantalize us with hints of a beautiful future somewhere, which we have decided to call "heaven."

The first pointer is the best: Without mentioning heaven, Jesus spoke of his Father's house with its many rooms. And then he told his disciples he would come again and get them, so that they could be with him (John 14:2, 3). And then we have Jesus praying that his disciples would be with him to see his glory (John 17:24). There is Paul saying we are now citizens of heaven (Phil. 3:20), and that we have a hope laid up in heaven (Col. 1:5). Peter reminds his Christian friends that their inheritance is kept in heaven for them (1 Peter 1:4). And then there is John reporting, "I heard what seemed to be the loud voice of a great multitude in heaven" (Rev. 19:1). Maybe the closest to a direct indicator of a future home is 2 Corinthians 5:1. The apostle continues his discussion of the eternal state by referring to the new house God has prepared for us "eternal in the heavens." And that's about it! It's not very much, but it's clear that heaven is worth waiting for.

* * *

What I've said above explains why some theologians have been cautious about the pronouncements they make about heaven. I appreciate that caution; it is much better than the Muslim imagination that the virgins are waiting in heaven for the young fighters killed in war or the less exotic prediction I have heard at funerals, "John is now enjoying better pizza than he ever had on earth." Unfortunately, many of our discussions reveal such crudely materialistic thinking. It is probably such thoughtless excesses that led Stanley Grenz to use "heaven" quite sparingly as he discusses our future of bliss in "the new creation" (pp. 644-49). The Bible uses "space" and "place" words to speak of the eternal realm. However, the central focus always is on the nature of life in eternity. I will try to observe the same cautions as I list the ten ways in which the concluding creative act of God will make all things new; and I will call it heaven as we are used to doing it.

1. The most important feature of the new life is that God will be there. This is the key to the system; without God it would not be heaven. Heaven is the community of those who live in fellowship with God and get happiness out of it because they have decided to love God. The Israelite community in the wilderness was taught to think of God as living in the back room of the big tent in the center of the encampment. He was there, but distinctly separate. The prophet Ezekiel has a poignant vision of God leaving the temple because the people had used it for idolatry (Ez. 10). Our experience now may be somewhat like that. We believe he is with us but he seems remote. We may wonder where he has gone. But in heaven he will dwell with us permanently (1 Thess. 4:17), not apart by himself behind a thick veil but so near that we will know him as he is (1 John 3:2). Philosopher Richard Swinburne suggests "God will be present to the inhabitants of heaven as intimately as their own thoughts" (Freddoso, p. 41).

2. The life of heaven will be a life of glory. "Glory" is one of the most used words in the Bible and one of the least understood. God is the God of glory and in heaven we will share that glory. In 1 Corinthians 15 the apostle has a thorough analysis of the future resurrection. He does not mention heaven but he sees that in our future we will have a new imperishable body. This will be a body of glory and power. It will be a spiritual body. Paul expects this will be a puzzler, so he repeats the affirmation, "Just as surely as there now are physical bodies, there will then be spiritual bodies." At this present point we are still people of the dust, as Adam was. But then we will "bear the image of the man of heaven," meaning we will be like the resurrected, heavenly Jesus in his glory (v. 42-49).

3. Heaven will be without sorrow, pain, or death. This is impressed upon us by the repeated promise that "God will wipe away every tear from their eyes" (Rev.7:17, 21:4). This is probably a figurative way of saying that there will be nothing in that life that will ever cause tears. "For the first things have passed away." The old way of nature that has ruled our lives throughout history will be a thing of the past. Finally, the writer of the Revelation reports that "nothing accursed will be found there anymore" (22:3). When Adam and Eve sinned the ground was cursed. We have all lived under the dark shadow of that curse. Eventually that curse will be erased.

The saddest feature of this present life is that it always involves dying. Jesus wept at the tomb where his friend was buried. Paul speaks of death as the last enemy to be destroyed (1 Cor. 15:26). The compassionate pastor who wrote Hebrews speaks of "those who all their lives were held in slavery by the fear of death" (Heb. 2:15). In the eternal system of things there will be no dying. We have been given a preview of this in the earthly work of Jesus. He healed the sick, stopped the storms, fed the hungry, expelled evil spirits from their human hosts, and raised the dead. He did not wipe out all problems, but enough to give us an idea how God will go about making bad things right. With his life he gave notice to us and the powers of darkness that he is indeed Lord over all of creation. The suffering that shows up every now and then in all of our lives will never appear again in the eternal system of things.

4. Heaven will be without sin. There won't be any evil in the entire environment. Revelation has two lists of sins that will never enter heaven (21:8, 27). These represent the whole, ugly batch. I'm surprised that cowardice is at the head of the list. Being cowardly seems like a mental weakness, rather than a sin against God. But this is Revelation, written for the persecuted Christians of the first century. Throughout, two kinds of loyalty have been pictured. You either have the Father's name on your forehead or the mark of the beast. In other words, you will either bow to God or salute the Empire. The Christian life entails conflict. Cowardice is choosing the safety of the world rather than the risks of following Jesus. Denying Christ for safety's sake is the first trait that will never show up in heaven.

I note that lying or dishonesty is mentioned in both lists. God's entire adventure of straightening this world is a matter of confronting deception and dishonesty with truth. The devil is the father of all lying (John 8:44); God is the author of all truth. When Jesus stood up to the Roman governor Pontius Pilate he declared, "I came into the world to testify to the truth" (John 18:37). He was on a truth mission. Revelation says he accomplished what he came to do. In the end truth will gain the victory and heaven will be a society of honesty.

5. Heaven will be a life of peace. We know about the struggles that are innate to all human life, the struggle against relentless temptations, against spells of bleak and black depression, against nameless fears and anxieties, against horrible maladies that will disfigure us and kill us, against the contempt and scorn we receive simply because we are different, against the hate we receive for being loyal to the Lord of love. But throughout the Holy Scriptures there is the hope that God's people can overcome. They may be martyred for their faith, they may toil in poverty, they may never feel triumphant, but by God's grace they can overcome. Those who overcome will inherit heaven (Rev. 21:7), and there they will be at peace.

6. Our life in heaven will consist of service. This is promised without any explanation or elaboration, "and his servants will serve him" (Rev. 22:3). We can wonder and imagine and dream what that service will be like. Some translations say "his servants will worship him." Humans were made for service. The highest satisfactions in life are gained through worshipful service. It thrills the soul to offer some service to God, not for praise or reward but out of loyalty and gratitude. It will be no different in heaven. We will serve, and we will be enriched by our serving, because that is the purpose for which we were created.

7. In heaven we will experience rest. When Jesus promised rest for weary and burdened souls he was probably not thinking of heaven (Matt. 11:28-30). He meant that following him into the work of the kingdom would be a good life because he was a gentle master. When Hebrews 4:9-11 promises that "those who enter God's rest will cease from their labors" it is not heaven that is in view. The promise is for those who are willing

to let go of their attachment to the rules of the first covenant and submit in trust and loyalty to Jesus, the Messiah. Earlier in this chapter I quoted the professor who hopes there will be opportunity for rest alongside of all the exciting new activity. And the promise finally comes in Revelation 14:13, "Blessed are the dead who from now on die in the Lord." "Yes," says the Spirit, "they will rest from their labors, for their works follow them." The last line probably does not mean that we will arrive in heaven with a list of our hard-won accomplishments that we can post somewhere for heavenly visitors to admire. It likely means we will arrive there as the new people that we have become by God's grace. It is not successful work that will count at the gates to heaven but the new Christ-shaped character. Swinburne's view "is that heaven is not a reward for good action . . .; rather it is a home for good people" (Freddoso), p. 43.

8. Heaven will feel like home. In Robert Frost's "Death of the Hired Man" the speaker says, "Home is the place, where when you have to go there, they have to let you in." What he means in his bitterness is that the hired man should go home to die; that's where he belongs. The Christian version of this is that when *we are dead* we go home to heaven because that's where *we* belong. The "home" metaphor is often used at funerals. In 2 Corinthians 5:6-8 the alternatives are set before us; we are either at home in the body or at home with the Lord. Humans once had a home, Eden. They were sent away because they did not fit in anymore. Since then we have all been like Cain, homeless wanderers. The innate longing I have mentioned at several points could be seen as the universal desire to get back home. As Hebrews 13:14 has it, "Here we have no lasting city." The fictitious Thomas Hardy character says, "The main business of religion is not to get a man into heaven but to get heaven into him." Once that happens one will feel totally at home there.

9. In heaven we will be what we were meant to be. Heaven is the Bible's answer to the incompleteness we see around us (1 Cor 13:8-10). The apostle John confesses that even though we are already God's children "what we will be has not yet been revealed." However, we will be like God once we see him (1 John 3:2). We will be like our Lord in love, honesty, and sincerity. There we will finally be free to deal with all habits of anger, envy, unforgiveness, and hypocrisy. The Croatian theologian Miroslav Volf suggests somewhere that we might as well

learn to live with our enemies and embrace them in love now because in heaven we'll be doing that anyway. Jesus' vision for his people was that they would abide in love, just as he abides in the Father's love. That would be a settled, permanent relationship of love and loyalty.

10. This brings me to my last point: Heaven will be an endless life of growth, quest, and becoming. Of all the nice things one can say about heaven, I have found this meets with most resistance from good folks. They have been taught to think that in heaven we will instantly be perfect. And that will be that. You realize by now this is not where this book has been taking you. And I hope you realize that it would not be how God works with his creation, the people whom he has made in his image. He loves them, challenges them to loyalty and trust, offers his forgiveness, promises to be with them, and reminds them his plan is that they grow to resemble Jesus. That's what our earthly pilgrimage has been all about. And I see no reason why that should be different in eternity. I expect it will be an endless adventure of learning, growing, shedding bad earthly habits, finally finding the freedom to admit all sins, expanding spiritually under the unlimited resources of God's grace, and rejoicing eternally in the fellowship of the Lord who has brought us through trouble and toil to be with him. Volf says it with these profound and beautiful words, "The whole creation along with human beings will be freed from transience and sins to reach the state of eternal peace and joy in the communion with the Triune God" (Polkinghorne, p. 278).

* * *

Expecting heaven is good for us. Some pessimists have suggested that hoping for a better future cheats a person out of the existential happiness of the present. They may speak sarcastically of those who are blind to the troubles around them and just wait for "pie in the sky." It need not be so. A solid hope is itself the source of happiness. It is the pleasure of expectation that makes life good, and worth the living.

As I have occasionally mentioned, many of us find this present life unfulfilling; it doesn't meet our deepest longings. This is probably a sign we have been designed for a better, higher world.

However, C. S. Lewis says many find it difficult to look forward to heaven because it seems unreal. Talk about eternity and heaven seems strangely outmoded to the modern thinker. The present physical world in this time we know. This is the only reality one has experienced. Heaven is by definition outside of our experience. But all talk about it must use this-earthly language. The Spirit could only reveal the truth about heaven to the prophets and apostles through words and concepts we use on earth. In other words, our words may not really fit the other-worldly reality that we try to describe.

Another reason many have no appetite for the world of the future is that this stuff about white robes and thrones and golden crowns and palm branches is impossible to take seriously. So, they shrug off the promises of an eternal future by facetiously rejecting the idea of spending eternity on a cloud with a harp. They fail – or refuse – to understand that all the scriptural imagery about heaven (as well as of hell) has to be taken figuratively. The next dimension can only be described for us in words and images that we use in this world. Lewis concludes that people who take these heavenly images literally might as well think that when Christ told us to be like doves he meant that we were to lay eggs (*Mere Christianity*, p. 131).

One of the basic dictums with which I have worked is that a strong hope allows one to enjoy the future blessings before they arrive. We can enjoy a foretaste of heaven while still on earth. We can commit ourselves to the duties of life without anxiety about death and the uncertainties about the hereafter. Further, among the many signs of a lively faith and hope in eternal life, one of the surest is not being overly sad at the death of those whom we love in the Lord. In the hour of death, hope allows us to let go serenely.

The author of *The Letter to the Hebrews* inserts a delightful reference to the motivational effects of hope in his chapter on faith. He wants his readers to join him in the life of faith (Heb. 10:39). Since they seem to be tempted to return to their former religious traditions, he reminds them that their old spiritual heroes, Abel, Enoch, Noah, Abraham, and Sarah were all people of faith in their day. Because they believed, they could obey God when obedience seemed problematic. They could live in trust even when there was no evidence their trust would be rewarded. They walked with God even when the going was tough. He explains how they did it; they were looking ahead in faith. What they anticipated is called a city with foundations, built for them by God, a homeland, and a better, heavenly country (11:10, 13-16). Old Testament believers rarely looked ahead to heaven; some scholars say they never did; their future was simply to be in s*heol,* the underworld. But this New Testament writer looks at the past and sees believers who were inspired by a strong faith in heaven. We wonder where they got their information; there is no mention of a God-designed city or of a new homeland in the narratives of Genesis. And we wonder how this writer knew about their hope. I think we have to assume the early people had some important information that did not get into the written narratives.

The reference to the future city with foundations is fascinating. You see, in the early times described in the Genesis narratives important men built cities. It started with Enoch (Gen. 4:17). With a city they made a name for themselves. Cities with walls provided security for their posterity. Abraham had left a good city, Ur in Babylon. In Canaan he and his descendants pastured their herds in a land dotted by small cities. But they had no home city; they lived in tents on land they did not own. They could have felt inferior as homeless nomads. But they were encouraged to walk with God because he would have a city for them at the end.

For us, hoping can be enhanced by a careful reading of John's Gospel. Jesus frequently spoke about eternal life. Sometimes it's simply "life" (John 3:15, 16, 10:28). This is the life of eternity. It's a new quality of living. People who have this life still die, as all others do. But in a sense, they already have one foot in eternity even as they keep on living here. Eternal life means they already have a home in heaven.

For the apostle Paul the hope of heaven is based only on the resurrection of Jesus. All of 1 Corinthians 15 was written to strengthen and solidify the hope of a future in heaven. He declares that if Christ has not been raised there is no faith and no hope. Christ was raised to be the firstfruits, or the prototype, of all others who are going to heaven. He tries to explain what the heavenly life will be like. But he finds it almost impossible; he tries many metaphors and symbols. At the end he simply says, "Just look at Jesus. The new kind of life he had after the resurrection is a model of how it will be for us" (v. 45-49).

Now, one more reminder of how it will be. Revelation speaks of two important actors on the stage of history – the Lion and the Lamb. As we read through the visions we soon discover they represent the same character, Jesus Christ. He is called the Lion in 5:5, but always after that, twenty-six times, he is the Lamb. This is meant to remind us that God's reclamation of the created world is not being achieved through ruthless power and brute strength, but through a gentle, sacrificial love. God's redemptive work is lamb-like. One might have thought that at the end of the drama Christ would emerge again, triumphantly, as the Lion. But no, in the two chapters that visualize the end (21, 22) Christ is still, consistently, the Lamb. We are not to forget that what we will receive at the end is not gained because we have run so fast or worked so hard. We have been rescued because Jesus in his death of sacrifice has reclaimed all of God's creation. It is because of the Lamb that there is heaven for people. Further, the central presence of the Lamb in the eternal community (22:3) reminds us that his gracious, sacrificial way of creating new people out of us sinners continues on in eternity. He is still the Lamb!

With its last two chapters the Revelation concludes as many other books do, "And they lived happily ever after." Every fairy tale and every romance that closes with that secular benediction is an expression of the deep-set human need for a happy conclusion to every story. Here it is again, the ending to transcend all endings. But as soon as those words are before me in print I recognize that I must amend myself. Actually, this is no ending at all; this is the beginning of the *real* story. I now express that conviction with the eloquent words of C. S. Lewis as he concludes the final book of his Narnia series, *The Last Battle*:

> The things that began to happen after that were so great and beautiful
> that I cannot write them.
> And for us this is the end of all stories, and we must truly say that they lived happily ever after.
> But for them it was only the beginning of the real story.
> All their life in this world and all their adventures in Narnia had only been the cover and the title page:
> now at last they were beginning Chapter One of the Great Story which no one on earth has read: which goes on forever; in which every chapter is better than the one before (p. 171).

Jesus once said something about praise coming from the lips of infants. Two grandsons were having lunch with us. The six-year-old was rambling on and on in his blossoming childhood wisdom. "There's lots of people in the world. And there's lots of Christians in the world too. Did you know that, Grandpa? Do you think they will all have room in heaven?" His seven-year-old brother, munching his broccoli, leaned over and informed him softly, "God can make heaven bigger." I quietly applauded his insight. Let's not worry about heaven. We can leave that in God's hands. If this chapter puzzles you, please don't spend too much energy worrying about it. God will do it his way and that will be good.

### For Further Thought and Study

*1. When you have thought of heaven what aspect of it did you most anticipate? What has troubled you?*

*2. How difficult is it to accept the concept of living in heaven in contrast to just being there?*

*3. Why does the Bible, describing heaven, not even try to inform us about the ordinary features of life such as food, clothing, climate, means of travel, and most importantly for some, will we have pets there?*

*4. Survey the ten features of heaven mentioned in the chapter above. Which is most important to you? Which is hard to envision?*

*5. How attractive do you find the concept of heaven being a growing, changing, developing experience?*

*6. Read I Corinthians 15:35-49. At the end, who is the "man of heaven" and who are "those who are of heaven"?*

*7. In what way does the hope of heaven affect or influence the way you live now?*

# 13. Hope for the Coming of Jesus

*A faith in Christ without expectation of a Parousia is like a flight of stairs that leads nowhere, but ends in the void.* –Emil Brunner

*The second coming of Christ will be so revolutionary that it will change every aspect of life on this planet.* – Billy Graham

*We long for the coming kingdom not so much because we look for compensation for the pain and deficiencies of life on earth, but because we look for the fulness of what we already joyfully experience in Christ.* –Stephen Travis

*This Jesus, who has been taken up from you into heaven, will come in the same way as you saw him go into heaven* (Acts 1:11).

*So Christ, having been offered once to bear the sins of many, will appear a second time, not to deal with sin, but to save those who are eagerly waiting for him* (Heb. 9:28).

Everybody loves the idea of an Apocalypse. Fantastic imaginations about the end of the world, the more pressingly imminent the better, have always garnered enthusiastic popular interest. It hasn't always been a healthy interest. For as long as we've enjoyed this earth there have been morose and righteous sects of one sort or another telling us that Doomsday is just around the next corner. Any day now the universe will be shut down forever; the world in flame and fire will dissolve into nuclear dust, time will end, life will evaporate into nothingness, and all will be dead and cold. Whether produced by Hollywood's movie moguls or shouted out by passionate TV preachers, the shuddering thrill of the holocaust to come, the melodrama of the scenario, has been lapped up by people always looking for a new excitement to brighten up a banal life.

In religious circles it is called "eschatology," the study of the last things. Religious speculations have focused on the ride of the four apocalyptic horsemen (Rev. 6), the identity of the Anti-Christ who is seen as the great end-time enemy, the signs of the times, and setting the precise year and day when Christ will show up again. The appetite for ever newer and more titillating details about the Tribulation, Death, Judgment, Hell and Heaven seems to be insatiable. And it has been the source of enormous profits for those who had the gall and the greed to take advantage of their thrill-hungry audiences.

For evangelical people who respect the Bible, the popular term that wraps up all things of the future is the "second coming." Preaching and writing about the second coming of Jesus has not always been done with discretion either. In 1970 Hal Lindsey published *The Late Great Planet Earth* in which he suggested Jesus would likely return in 1988. By 1990 the book had sold 28 million copies. Edgar Whisenant had more precise insight. On September 11, 1988, I stood before a congregation with his booklet in my hands, and told them that if the author was correct most of them would likely not be present next Sunday, because Jesus was scheduled to appear between September 11 and 13. I assured them I was planning to preach the following Sunday anyway. I believe it was in 2002 that I was in a Christian bookstore, looking over their array of books on the last days. In one section a whole row of recent publications proclaimed that Saddam Hussein of Iraq was indeed the Antichrist of the end times. However, within a few years Hussein was in prison awaiting trial, Iraq was in shambles, and every one of those books was obsolete. All this is only a small fraction of the errors through which I have groaned over the course of my teaching/preaching life.

Surveying the havoc that the end-times industry has created with the hope of Jesus' return, one might not guess that the biblical witness to Jesus' next coming is actually quite concise, careful, and consistent. Jesus shared a detailed preview of his return with his disciples when they wondered what he meant with his words about the destruction of Jerusalem's temple (Matt. 24, Mark 13, Luke 21). It was graphic but also strangely inconclusive, because it was couched in figurative images borrowed from the Old Testament and the Jewish Apocalyptic literature of the times. The advice throughout is that the disciples are to remain sober minded, to watch carefully, and be ready at all times because no one knows when *that* time will come (Matt. 24:36).

The apostle Paul's most detailed study of the return of Jesus can be found in 1 Thessalonians 4:13-5:11. These words are easier to interpret than those of Jesus. He has the same pastoral concern that Jesus had, stay awake and keep sober. I think that probably means we should not be too excited or too indifferent about it all. Twice the apostle treats the hope of Jesus' coming as news that should motivate us to live courageously in the mean time (4:18, 5:11).

The letter to the Hebrew Christians mentions that when Christ comes for the second time it will be to save those who are waiting for him (9:28). This was meant to encourage these new believers who had become apprehensive about their loyalty to Jesus. After the author has reminded them how privileged they are with their new heavenly connections (12:22-24) he goes on to mention the end of this world. He does not use the images of Jesus or Paul, but speaks of it as a final "shake-up" (12:25-29). But that should not frighten them either, because they now belong to a "kingdom that cannot be shaken."

Peter informs his friends that the "day of the Lord" will not come with a flood, as it once did. What we can expect next time around is the fiery termination of this world. However, it is important to notice that this is not meant as a fearful threat because the end result will be a new world in which "righteousness is at home" (2 Peter 3:8-13).

Strangely, when we scan the final book of the Bible, the book of Revelation, we find no report about the return of Jesus. At the end, when the holy city comes from heaven to earth we are just informed that God is now here. The interpretation of the last two chapters hangs on the words of the angel who explains that the magnificent city at the center of this section represents the church of Jesus Christ (21:9, 10). After the church arrives on the new earth the loud voice calls out, "See, the home of God is among mortals. He will dwell with them as their God; they will be his people, and God himself will be with them" (Rev. 21:3). Later we are reminded once more that the Lord God Almighty and the Lamb reside in the church (21:22, 23).

Several New Testament writers refer to the return of Jesus as "the day of the Lord." This term is borrowed from the Old Testament where it is often used, not of a particular day, but of an approaching time when God will express his anger over Israel's unbelief in some fearful way. However, in the New Testament this Day is seen as a time of liberation and joy.

Theologians sometimes discuss the coming of Jesus as the coming of the kingdom of God. With this they don't contradict what I explained in Chapter 11, about the kingdom having arrived on earth with the first coming of Jesus. *That* kingdom is now here and we are invited to join the kingdom and work for its world-wide growth. They mean that the kingdom to which we belong now will then attain its ultimate completion. In other words, there is an "already" aspect to the kingdom as well as a "not yet." The full realization of the kingdom of God, which will involve the resurrections, the final judgments, the conclusion of this earthly, temporal era, the transformation of the physical world, and the inauguration of the ultimate, eternal era are all, somehow, effected by the coming of Jesus.

What I am maintaining is that the New Testament is through and through goal-oriented. Repeatedly, in almost every writing, there is the forward look, the anticipation of the return of the Lord Jesus at the end of the age. The God events of the past, from creation at the beginning to the resurrection of Jesus, cannot be correctly interpreted or fully understood until Jesus returns. That will be like the last chapter in the mystery novel. Then we will lean back and exclaim, "Aha, so this is what the story is all about!"

The popular term, "the second coming" is never used in the Bible. The closest to it is the promise in Hebrews 9:28 that Jesus "will appear a second time." That line can serve as the introduction to the language used to describe the promise of Jesus' return. You see, after Jesus had completed his earthly, physical mission and was preparing to leave he assured his disciples that he would actually be with them till the end of this age. He is now here, everywhere, wherever, invisibly. One day the invisible one will appear and be visible again. Six times his return is given simply as an appearing, as becoming visible. "And every eye will see him" (Rev. 1:7).

The most common word that the New Testament writers use of Jesus' return is *parousia.* It is used about fifteen times of Jesus and some preachers have used it as *the* technical term for his coming. Dictionaries say it connotes both a coming and a presence. Jesus is coming to be with us. The other word that is used a few times of Jesus is *apokalupsis,* which suggests an uncovering or a revealing.

The coming of the Lord has sometimes been preached as a threat. Like, "It will be too late to repent when you hear the blast of the heavenly trumpet." The warning may be as ominous as the dark words we remember from childhood when we were guilty of some stubborn mischief, "Just wait till Daddy gets home." The parable of Matthew 24:45-51 lends itself to this kind of fear-mongering. However, the general New Testament approach to the coming of Jesus is a joyful expectation.

The New Testament hope for the return of Jesus has nothing to do with any this-worldly events. Our hope is not based on any rearrangements of the world's political power blocks, by the desecration of nature, by technological advances, by movements of religious revival, or by the accumulation of greater and more sinister expressions of human evil. Any one of these has been touted as a sure "sign of the times." I've heard them all. Jesus *did* speak of signs (Matt.24:3), but they were the marks of the age that he had inaugurated with his first coming; he was describing what the world of the disciples would be like after he would leave. The disciples needed to know that there would be hard times ahead for them. No Paradise yet! Later in the same lecture he emphasized that his next coming was known only by the Father (Matt. 24:36). So, instead of studying social developments, religious trends, political movements, global climate change, or the explosion of global communication networks for signs that Jesus is at the door, just keep busy for the Lord (Matt. 24:46). Mark's version of Jesus' end-times lecture (Ch. 13) concludes with the ringing call to beware, keep alert, be on the watch, and keep awake (Mark 13:32-37). Children who have heard this have sometimes been afraid to go to bed. A minister whose testimony I read recently said as a teenager he had slept in his clothes for months in order to be ready to join Jesus at a moment's notice. Hopefully we can go on from such naïve sincerity to appreciate the *real* truths that Jesus' figurative language is meant to convey.

Even though Jesus' teaching was touched by futuristic concepts, he did not advocate flight from the here and now. But he did direct his disciples to keep looking ahead. Without the hereafter the present would lose its meaning. In fact, our vision of the future may have a stronger directive influence on our lives than the experiences of the past. Those with a clear hope of life in heaven hereafter will not be content to live in hell now. As 1 Corinthians 13:12 has it, this present life is like seeing someone's reflection in a dark mirror; we are looking forward to seeing each other face to face.

* * *

This may be the place to address a wonder that may be troubling you. Why have some of your treasured convictions not received any attention in my writing? How is it that I see things in the Scriptures that other authors have not noticed? Why is it that our end-times hope, especially, has so many potential variations? Why do people who sincerely try to be biblical disagree with one another about what is to come? My answer here is not a defense of my convictions but an explanation of how listening to the Bible works.

1. The Bible does not present us with a unified, systematic message of hope, but witnesses to hope at many points and in many different ways.

2. The material about the future is scattered throughout the Scriptural writings. There is a chapter that deals comprehensively with love (1 Cor. 13), a chapter on the resurrection (1 Cor. 15), a chapter on faith (Heb. 11), and so on. But there is no book or chapter that gives us a complete analysis of what will happen at the end. So, the material that we collect from here and there can be assembled in different ways.

3. Details about the eternal dimension of human life have to be described in this-worldly language and that leads to variations in interpretation because we come to the Bible from many different backgrounds.

4. Much of the Bible, especially that which is predictive, is given in symbolic language and in poetic form, and needs to be read with that in mind.

5. There is the difficulty, in both Testaments, of deciding what has immediate and localized significance and what speaks of the end in a general way.

6. And then there are human factors that stand in the way of a unified understanding. There is the temptation to make the Bible say more than it says. In other words, human curiosity desires more information than divine revelation has disclosed.

7. The problem above is intensified by the assumption that end-times material is given to provide us with information, when the divine purpose may rather be to produce hope and holy living.

8. And then there is the rather common human inclination towards passionate dogmatism on matters about the end times; such hot-headedness tends to wreck all careful thinking.

* * *

Heeding the dangers listed above, we should be able to agree at least on the following aspects of Jesus' next coming. First, it will be unexpected. Jesus warned, "Keep alert, for you do not know when the time will come" (Mark 13:33). To that the apostle adds that the day of the Lord will come like a thief in the night. When people will think all is safe and secure "then sudden destruction will come upon them" (1 Thess. 5:3). Both Jesus and Paul seem to say that for the believer who is ready the coming of Jesus will not be a surprise.

Secondly, the coming of Jesus is always near. Theologians speak of the Lord's imminent coming. Others think it would be more precise to say his return is impending. The apostle reminded his friends in Rome that "the night is far gone, the day is near" (Rom. 13:12). "Night" is a symbol for ignorance, sin, and confusion, "the day" is occasionally used as shorthand for the Day of the Lord. The New Testament position is that since the death, resurrection, and ascension of Jesus the return is always near.

Thirdly, Christ's next appearing will be a public event. Jesus had a humble birth in a cattle shed, his work was confined to one of the least auspicious provinces of the Empire, and when he died he was still relatively unknown. However, when he shows up again it will be like the lightning that flashes across the whole sky from east to west. (Matt. 24:27). So obvious will be the coming of Jesus. Mark announces that Jesus will come in the clouds with great power and glory (Mark 13:26). And then Revelation 1:7 announces that "every eye will see him." These are dramatic, picturesque images borrowed from the Old Testament. The writers seem to get carried away as they seek to verbalize what will be glorious beyond the powers of human expression.

Fourthly, it will *not* be like the arrival of a furious, blood-thirsty conqueror. I add this corrective point because of how too many of my biblical colleagues have interpreted Revelation 19:11-16. That particular vision has Christ riding throughout the world on a white charger and striking down the nations with his sword. It is assumed that the peace-loving Savior will return as a furious, vengeful executioner. What is overlooked by readers who are lusting for bloody holy vengeance is that the rider's name is "The Word of God" and that the sword comes out of his mouth. In view of the image's location in the drama and of how spiritual truths are physically visualized throughout Revelation, it is likely meant to depict the Lord's worldwide crusade against the lies and deceptions of the devil. Jesus called his opponent, the devil, "the father of lies" (John 8:44). He assured his disciples, "I am the way, the truth, and the life" (John 14:6). When on trial for blasphemy he told Pilate, the Roman strongman, "For this I came into the world, to testify to the truth" (John 18:37). The figurative images of Revelation 19 are a report on the success of Christ's truth crusade. At the end no lies or falsehood will be left (Rev. 21:8, 27). This leads me now to the conclusion of this chapter and this book. It is closure time. This is how the earthly part of the human story concludes.

I have often spoken of the end. Now I must clarify that there actually is no end to God's big love project. What is concluded is God's temporary creation of a human community on a physical earth. It will be wrapped up by Christ's return. First, Christ's return will complete the work of rescuing humankind from the bondage and the environment of sin. The freedom of which every believer has at least a taste already (discussed in Ch. 7), will then be fully and gloriously realized. Full salvation!

Secondly, the return of Christ will involve the unveiling of all that is so far kept in the shadows. We will then see and understand Christ as he is (1 John 3:2). Through the end-time judgments it will also be revealed who we are. For some this may be a painful and disappointing experience. On the other hand, it may be an exhilarating epiphany as the light of heaven reveals who we really are. "Therefore judge nothing before the appointed time; wait until the Lord comes. He will bring to light what is hidden in darkness and will expose the motives of men's hearts. At that time each will receive his praise from God" (1 Cor. 4:5, NIV).

Christ came originally to help people out of the evil mess into which the great enemy of God had sucked everybody. We often wonder how that project is doing. Is the devil backing down and losing influence as the Holy Spirit and Spirit-filled people confront and oppose the evil one? There are many local skirmishes that God's people seem to win, but what about the big conflict? How is God's cause doing? As we wonder about that, the Scriptures assure us that eventually Christ will be unequivocally victorious. Eventually he will hand the kingdom of God over to the Father, "after he has destroyed every ruler and every authority and every power. For he must reign until he has put all his enemies under his feet" (1 Cor. 15:24, 25). Without the hope of this final victory over evil, the huge question of why the Creator allowed his beautiful world to be invaded by sin would remain an eternal mystery. There will not be an ongoing, directionless conflicting struggle between good and evil throughout eternity. Christ will return to end all evil so that God's order of beauty and goodness may again prevail.

Fourth, Christ will come to bring the human history of this era to a conclusion. In the first place, and most obviously, it will mean the end of all dying. Death is a very unfriendly reality. It has often been pointed out that while the dying person may not realize what is happening, it sure is hard on the survivors. That suffocating cloud of grief will have no place in the eternal world. I wonder, how will the dark and dreadful experiences of this time be remembered? Will they even exist in our memories? I don't know. Anyway, the good news is that those who have died and are already with Christ will show up in bodies that are imperishable (that will not age) and then those who are still alive will be transformed into the same kind of new bodies. Together they will laugh and rejoice at this final victory over their earthiness. Read about it in 1 Corinthians 15:50-57. It is important to understand that this will not be an inferior form of living. This will be real life, full life, complete life. The Swedish theologian Gustaf Aulen reminds us we are not anticipating an "inert immutability" that will consist only of peace and rest. We will live with God in a life that is "characterized by a divinely motivated activity" (p. 446).

Fifth, Christ will return, not only to change humans for life in the eternal kingdom but to transform the entire universe as well. This will be the new heaven and earth of Revelation 21:1 that I have already discussed in Chapter 11. The universe, together with its human population will be set free from its bondage to decay (Rom. 8:21). It is difficult for us to imagine how this may be, but the least we can say is that it will be totally different from how we have learned to understand physical matter. Peter says righteousness will be at home in that new world (2 Peter 3:13). Those cryptic words simply mean it's all going to be good, forever.

Finally, Jesus our Lord will come to consummate his fellowship with his followers. If there would not be an event such as is suggested by the many references to Christ's appearing we would at the end be left with a cry of anguish, "So what?" As Emil Brunner suggests, life would then have been like toiling up a long staircase that, at the end, goes nowhere. For many of us life has been good. Our trust relationship with Jesus has inspired us to hope even when things looked hopelessly dark. We have carried on with heads held high and a smile on our lips when circumstances might have destroyed us. As the apostle says, we are afflicted, crushed, perplexed, persecuted, but we carry on by the power of Jesus who lives in us (2 Cor. 4:8-11). But even the messenger of such a triumphant courage admits, "If for this life only we have hoped in Christ, we are of all people most to be pitied" (1 Cor. 15:19). It is the hope of a new and better life in the future that allows us to live thankfully in the present. I refer once more to the wisdom of Gustaf Aulen, "Christian hope receives both its assurance and its richness in the encounter of faith with the sovereign, creative love of God." But in spite of that warm assurance created in us by God's love, we conclude that "the content of life eternal is so ineffable that faith is unable to speak of it in any other forms than groping figures" (p. 447).

All that is left then is the wonder. How can all this be? How will I respond when I am invited into a life that is at this point completely beyond my comprehension? How long will it be before I'll feel comfortable in that new strangeness? Will I find out that, in spite of my best intentions, I've made mistakes in this book? If so, will I be allowed to confess? And to whom will I confess, my family, my friends, my Lord? Of one thing I'm quite certain, there will be complete forgiveness for any failures. We have already lived off God's forgiveness here. There will be no less grace in eternity. So, I leave you with this testimony of my hope and welcome you again to join me in my hoping. We expect the best is yet to come!

*For Further Thought and Study*

*1. Does the thought of Christ's return please you, confuse you, frighten you, or repulse you? Explain.*

*2. Compare some of the "Parousia" comments in the New Testament: Matthew 24:3, 1 Corinthians15:23, 1 Thessalonians 2:19, 3:13, 5:23, 2 Thessalonians 2:1, 2, James 5:7, 2 Peter 3:4, 1 John 2:28. What do you learn?*

*3. Read 1 Corinthians 15:50-57. What new insights does this text have for you? In what sense could the apostle call this a victory that God gives us (v. 57)?*

*4. After reading 1 Corinthians 15:50-57 turn to a parallel, 1 Thessalonians 4:13-17. How do you integrate these two accounts of the believer's experience with the coming of the Lord?*

*5. The apostle says the person who asks questions about our eternal bodies is a fool. But then he goes on to try an explanation anyway. What do you make of 1 Corinthians 15:35-44?*

*6. How useful are the author's eight points about interpreting end-time predictions?*

*7. Think through the list of the six effects of Christ's coming. Which will you appreciate the most? Why?*

# Resources That Have Been Consulted or Quoted

Atkinson, Basil F. C. *Life and Immortality*, 1969.

Augustine of Hippo. *Augustine's Confessions*. Grand Rapids: Sovereign Grace Publishers, 1971.

Aulen, Gustaf. *The Faith of the Christian Church*. Philadelphia: The Muhlenberg Press, 1948.

Baillie, John. *And the Life Everlasting*. London: Oxford University Press, 1934.

Beck, Richard. *The Slavery of Death*. Eugene: Cascade Books,2014.

Bernstein, Alan E. *The Formation of Hell*. London: UCL, 2003.

Blamires, Harry. *The God Who Acts*. Ann Arbor: Servant Books, 1981.

Bloesch, Donald. *The Last Things*. Downers Grove: InterVarsity, 2004.

Braaten, Carl E. *The Future of God*. New York: Harper and Row, 1969.

_____. and Jenson, Robert, eds. *The Last Things*. Grand Rapids: Eerdmans, 2002.

Brown, Colin, ed. *The New International Dictionary of New Testament Theology*, Vol.1-3. Grand Rapids: Zondervan, 1976.

Cooper, John W. *Body, Soul, and Life Everlasting*. Grand Rapids: Eerdmans, 1989.

Date, Christopher M. and Highfield, Ron, eds. *A Consuming Passion*. Eugene: Wipf and Stock Publishers, 2015.

Dearmer, Percy. *The Legend of Hell*. London: Casell & Company, 1929.

Edwards, David L. and Stott, John. *Essentials, A Liberal-Evangelical Dialogue*. London: Hodder and Stoughton, 1988.

Ellul, Jacques. *Hope in Time of Abandonment*. New York: The Seabury Press, 1972.

Fackenheim, Emil L. "The Commandment to Hope." *The Future of Hope*. Edited by Walter H. Capps. Philadelphia: Fortress Press, 1970.

Fackre, Gabriel. *The Christian Story*. Grand Rapids: Eerdmans, 1996.

Farrar, F. W. *Mercy and Judgment*. London: MacMillan and Co., 1881.

Freddoso, Alfred J., ed. *The Existence and Nature of God*. Notre Dame: University of Notre Dame Press, 1983.

Fudge, Edward William. *The Fire That Consumes*. Houston: Providential Press, 1982.

Gregg, Steve. *All You Want to Know about Hell.* Nashville: Thomas Nelson, 2013.

Grenz, Stanley. *Theology for the Community of God.* Grand Rapids: Eerdmans, 2000.

Grimsrud, Ted. *The Triumph of the Lamb.* Scottdale: Herald Press, 1987.

Guinness, Os. *Renaissance.* Downer's Grove: Inter Varsity Press, 2014.

Hanna, William, ed. *Letters of Thomas Erskine of Linlathen.* Edinburgh: David Douglas, 1878.

Harris, Murray. *Raised Immortal.* Grand Rapids: Eerdmans, 1983.

Hebblethwaite, Brian. *The Christian Hope.* Grand Rapids: Eerdmans, 1984.

Helm, Paul. *The Last Things: Death, Judgment, Heaven, Hell.* Edinburgh: The Banner of Truth Trust, 1989.

Hick, John. *Evil and the God of Love.* Glasgow: William Collins Sons, 1979.

Jersak, Bradley. *Her Gates Will Never Be Shut.* Eugene: Wipf & Stock, 2009.

_____. *A More Christlike God.* Pasadena: Plain Truth Ministries, 2015.

Jonathan, Stephen. *Grace Beyond the Grave.* Eugene: Wipf and Stock, 2014.

Jones, L. Gregory. *Embodying Forgiveness.* Grand Rapids: W. B. Eerdmans, 1995.

Kapic, Kelly M. *Embodied Hope.* Downers Grove: Inter Varsity Press, 2017.

Klassen, Randolph J. *What Does the Bible Really Say About Hell?* Telford, PA: Pandora Press U.S., 2001.

Kvanvig, Jonathan L. *The Problem of Hell.* New York: Oxford University Press, 1993.

Leckie, J. H. *The World to Come and Final Destiny.* Edinburgh: T. & T. Clark, 1918.

Lewis, C. S. *The Problem of Pain.* London: Harper Collins, 1998.

_____. *Mere Christianity.* New York: The MacMillan Company, 1952.

_____. *The Last Battle.* London: Harper Collins Publishers, 1990.

Lindbeck, George A. *The Nature of Doctrine.* London: SPCK, 1984.

Lohfink, Gerhard. *Is This All There Is?* Collegeville, MN: Liturgical Press, 2017.

MacDonald, George. *Life Essential: The Hope of the Gospel.* Wheaton: Harold Shaw Publishers, 1974.

MacKintosh, H. A. *Immortality and the Future.* London: Hodder and Stoughton, 1915.

McCullough, Matthew. *Remember Death.* Wheaton: Crossway Books, 2018.

Martindale, Wayne. *Beyond the Shadowlands.* Wheaton: Crossway Books, 2005.

McLaren, Brian. *The Last Word and the Word after That.* San Francisco: Jossey-Bass, 2005.

Moltmann, Jurgen. *Hope and Planning.* New York: Harper & Row, Publishers, 1971.

_____. *Sun of Righteousness, ARISE!* Minneapolis: Fortress Press, 2010.

_____. *The Theology of Hope.* New York: Harper & Row, Publishers, 1965.

Nichols, Terence. *Death and Afterlife.* Grand Rapids: Brazos Press, 2010.

Oden, Thomas. *The Transforming Power of Grace.* Nashville: Abingdon Press, 1993.

Odgers, James Edwin. "Universalism." *Encyclopedia of Religion and Ethics.*

Packer, J. I. "The Problem of Eternal Punishment." *Crux.* September, 1990, pp. 18-25.

Parry, Robin A., and Partridge, Christopher H., ed. *Universal Salvation?* Grand Rapids: Eerdmans, 2003.

Peters, Ted. *God – the World's Future.* Minneapolis: Fortress Press, 1992.

Polkinghorne, John, and Welker, Michael, ed. *The End of the World and the Ends of God.* Harrisburg: Trinity Press, 2000.

Reicke, Bo. *The Disobedient Spirits and Christian Baptism.* Kobenhavn: Ejnar Munksgaard, 1946.

Robinson, John A. T. *In the End, God .* London: James Clarke & Co., 1950.

Sasse, Herman. "aion, aionias." *Theological Dictionary of the Old Testament,* Vol. I.

Shedd, William G. T. *The Doctrine of Endless Punishment.* London: James Nisbet & Son, 1886.

Smith, James K. A. "Determined Hope: A Phenomenology of Christian Expectation." *The Future of Hope.* Edited by Miroslav Volf & William Katerberg. Grand Rapids: Eerdmans, 2004.

Swinburne, Richard. "A Theodicy of Heaven and Hell." *The Existence and Nature of God.* Edited by Alfred J. Freddoso. Notre Dame:University of Notre Dame Press, 1983.

Tiede, David. *Jesus and the Future.* Cambridge: Cambridge University Press, 1990.

Travis, Stephen. *The Jesus Hope.* Downers Grove: InterVarsity Press, 1974.

_____. *I Believe in the Second Coming of Jesus.* Grand Rapids: Wm. B. Eerdmans,1982.

Trumbower, Jeffrey. *Rescue for the Dead.* Oxford: Oxford University Press, 2001.

Tutu, Desmond. *God Has a Dream.* New York: Image Books, 2004.

Volf, Miroslav, and Katerberg, William, eds. *The Future of Hope.* Grand Rapids: Eerdmans, 2004.

Volf, Miroslav. *Free of Charge.* Grand Rapids: Zondervan, 2005.

Walls, Jerry L. *Heaven, Hell, and Purgatory.* Grand Rapids: Brazos Press, 2015

_____, *Heaven the Logic of Eternal Joy.* Oxford: University Press, 2002.

_____. *Hell: The Logic of Damnation.* Notre Dame: University of Notre Dame Press, 1992.

Wenham, John. "The Case for Conditional Immortality." Unpublished document, personal gift from the author, 1991.

Whale, J. S. *Victor and Victim*. Cambridge: Cambridge University Press, 1960.

Williams, Peter. *The Case for Angels*. Carlisle: Paternoster Press, 2002.

Wright, N. T. *Paul, A Biography*. San Francisco: HarperOne, 2018.

_____. *Surprised by Hope*. San Francisco: HarperOne, 2012.

_____. *The Day the Revolution Began*. San Francisco: HarperOne, 2016.

_____. "Universalism." *New Dictionary of Theology*.

Manufactured by Amazon.ca
Bolton, ON

10812153R00087